FROM DISCONNECT TO RECONNECT

A 12-Week Guide to Offline Freedom and Joy for Teens and Young Adults

You are enough!
LK Smith

By L.K. Smith

Copyright © 2018 L. K. Smith

All rights reserved. This book or any portion thereof
may not be reproduced or used in any manner whatsoever
without the express written permission of the author or publisher
except for the use of brief quotations in a book review.

Printed in the United States of America
First Printing, 2018

Author Website: www.lksmithauthor.com

Disclaimer
This book is designed to provide helpful information for parents, guardians,
teachers, teens and young adults. This book is not meant to be used, nor should
it be used, to diagnose or treat any medical or psychological condition. For
diagnosis or treatment of any medical or psychological problem, seek help from
your own physician or psychologist or other health professional.
All names and identifying details and characteristics have been
changed and are composites. Any likeness to actual persons is strictly
coincidental. The author and publisher have made every effort to ensure that
the information in this book was correct at press time, and do not assume any
liability to any party for any loss caused by errors or omissions, whether
from negligence, accident, or any other cause.

Credits
Cover and Book Design by Amy Livingstone
www.sacredartstudio.net

Editing by Linda M. Bendorf, Director, Blue Sage Writing
Author photograph by Jason Johnson

Library of Congress Control Number: 2018913873

ISBN: 978-0-578-41194-1

Dedicated to my DLCLGL 6 Tribe.
All my love, Mom

ABOUT THE AUTHOR

Parent. Teacher. Wife. Author. Teen Advocate. Linda Smith takes pride in being called "the teacher who hears them, really listens and teaches more than English. In 2016 Linda Smith won the Horace Mann Teacher of the Year Award. She has raised four fabulous children of her own, and has also worked with thousands of teens in her 25 years in the classroom. She demonstrates in her life and in her role as an educator the importance of reaching deep inside where our beautiful, amazing, authentic selves already exist, too often buried in the crush of social media and our unending hunger for validation. Smith knows that each one of us wants to be seen for the good we bring to the world, and that this can only happen when you invite *the real you*, your genius and all of your gifts to the surface. Since technology isn't going anywhere, Smith says, "We must change its role in our lives." This book will show you the path to inner joy and success, one small step at a time. Since everyone is unique, Smith does not call her book a "one-size fits all solution." Rather, throughout the book, she offers compelling examples from her own life and also composites of teens experiencing backlash from internet overuse or addiction; and step-by step exercises and options to lead your authentic self out of the social media rabbit hole to a life of true contentment. This book is her gift—her legacy—to teens, young adults, parents, guardians and teachers.

TABLE OF CONTENTS

PREFACE

Why I Wrote this Book. In the fall of 2017, I had what Professor Brené Brown refers to as a "spiritual awakening" at work. After a closed-door meeting where I completely lost my focus and my composure, I left the principal's office in deep, heavy, guttural sobs. I threw what I could into my book bag and headed out the door for home, tears stinging my cheeks as the autumn wind ripped through me. I was angry, embarrassed, ashamed and unsure like I never had been before. On my commute home, I played the victim over and over in my head. Self-pity overtook me as I pointed out everything that was wrong at school, how no one was listening to me, and how people must enjoy being stuck in the problem since they weren't interested in solving any of the issues my way.

A few hours later, I called a trusted friend who told me under no uncertain terms was I to send the resignation letter I had already drafted. That was the first blow to my ego. I then called my therapist who told me in the most compassionate way possible given my state of mind that I was wrong, and that I owed my principal an apology. What??? Later, my husband—who keeps me grounded like no one else—reiterated those words. I honestly felt like I had been slapped in the face by the people I love the most. In my head, I wanted to prove them all wrong. Couldn't they see I was the victim here? Who apologizes when they've been deeply wronged?

However, deep down in my heart, I knew they were right. Over the past several years, I have surrounded myself with honest, spiritual people who care enough to hold a mirror up to me when I most feel like smashing it. Oh sure, I knew I could call a few other people who would commiserate with me, tell me I was totally right, and that I should resign immediately.

But I am not a quitter.

And when I don't know what to do, I call the people who will be honest with me, and I ask for help. I have come to trust this group of individuals for guidance when I cannot see clearly. So I humbled myself, and I wrote a heartfelt apology to my principal. Her response was divine. Literally. She treated me with grace and mercy in a way I didn't know existed. She met my apology with a two week vacation and told me to do some soul-searching. And search I did.

After I explained to my younger children that mom had become too stressed out and needed some time off work, I set to task. I journaled, I prayed, I meditated, I had massages, I did yoga, I went to a chakra-energy healer, I took oil-infused hot baths, I sat on my front porch drinking herbal tea; I cooked clean, healthy organic foods; I napped, I took long walks in the trees behind our house. And I wept- sometimes uncontrollably.

What happened next, reminded me of a quotation by Rumi, a famous mystic and poet: "The wound is the place where the light enters you." Slowly, the sun emerged. Even though I spent a great deal of that time in fear and in tears, I learned a lot about myself and how I respond to stress. I questioned what I was doing in the classroom, and if I was having any effect anymore. I doubted my ability to walk back into my classroom and hold my head up. What started as one of the worst points of my life became a true watershed moment.

I began to define myself on my own terms. I am passionate about teenagers and love visiting with them about life's greatest challenges. I get just as excited as the kids do when we get off topic, because I get to really hear them. I can use my experience as a human, a mom, a wife, a teacher and a friend and show them how at the end of the day, we are all after the same things:

To feel we matter

To know we make a difference

We all want to know that we are heard and we are seen.

We want to know that once we're gone, we've left the world a better place.

I wrote *From Disconnect to Reconnect* because I felt compelled to do so. I knew in my heart that if I felt this way at 47 years old with a great husband, fabulous children, a stable environment, an awesome job, tremendous, honest friends...how are the kids in front of me feeling who may not have the experience and support systems in place that I do? Our teens have been tasked with the same milestones we had growing up - feeling awkward, not fitting in but trying desperately to do so, being unsure of our futures and our plans, not knowing if the decisions we made would come back and bite us later. Those inadequacies aren't new. However, today's young people have to contend with one exception: technology. I cannot tell you how many adults have said, "I am so glad we didn't have social media growing up. I would have died if people had a digital record of everything I did. I was allowed to make mistakes and my errors in judgment were forgotten over time."

Technology isn't going anywhere, so we have to change the manner and degree to which we infuse it into our lives. Today's teens are feeling much more pressure to fit in, to be ahead of everyone else, to be in constant competition with their best friends- whether verbalized or not.

As parents, teachers, role models, and pastors, we have to meet our kids in the middle. We have to give them the power to see themselves as the gifts they are.

Plain and simple, we cannot hand our kids a phone—Smart or otherwise—and walk away. We cannot think it's healthy for them to be digitally ruled. We must help to open their eyes to the dangers and drawbacks of social media, and offer coping skills, alternative activities, and authentic barometers for success. And while there is still the fear and the reality of someone stalking our children online, the real fear is that our kids are growing up feeling inadequate, stressed, anxious, and like they don't matter. It's up to us to give them the tools to dig deep and to find their value. Our youth need to know that they matter and that their lives have the potential to have a profound impact on others. We have to teach our kids how to unplug so that they can plug back into what matters: Life. Their goals, their ambitions, their passions, their purpose will not be fulfilled by staring at their screens. WE know this; but they don't. They may have only an inkling. It's up to us to help them to see the big picture and to help them on this journey, step by step. This is why I wrote this book.

Technology has its value and its place. No doubt about it. What we are ignoring is the fact that our kids are not learning how to cope in real time. They stuff their feelings deep down every time they scroll through a page, a post, a tweet, a message board, a forum. They look for their value and their worth based upon the external world. It's time for us to help them to literally disconnect so they can reconnect. To unplug so they can plug into what really matters.

Namasté,
L. K. Smith

A NOTE TO TEENS

Dear Friend,

Give yourself a high five for being here! To take an honest look at yourself and to want more out of your life are actions to be commended. You live in a world full of constant judgment: how many followers you have, how many likes, retweets, or comments you get. I have seen many a teen take a selfie over and over again just to get the right lighting or angle and then apply various filters in order to achieve "perfection." This habit breaks my heart. Why? Because each one of us is enough just as we are. But trying to convince you of this is like shoveling snow in a blizzard. I wrote this guide for any young adult who is struggling with image, desiring more out of life, or wishing to be fulfilled in the simplest of ways. Not everyone is going to be a YouTube phenom. And that's okay. What I do want for you is to be your own phenom, in your own unique way and on your own terms. Social media has kept you from your goals for far too long. I get it; when you read on, you will see how I, too, fell victim to the danger of looking for external validation.

I'm not advocating social media abstinence! We benefit from the disciplined and balanced use of social media. However, if you find you are addicted, it is critical to cut yourself off from social media for a period of time. How do you know if you're addicted? You will recognize yourself in the pages of this book.

I say from time to time in this book that I am not a psychologist, psychotherapist nor M.D., nor can I replace one, so if you are dealing with an ongoing problem or ongoing sadness or depression, SEEK IMMEDIATE HELP

- from a trusted adult
- or call the National Suicide Prevention Lifeline: 1-800-273-TALK (8255)
- or text 741741 from anywhere in the USA to text with a trained Crisis Counselor

Did you know that if you text 741741 when you are feeling depressed or suicidal, a crisis worker will text you back immediately and continue to text with you? Many people do not like talking on the phone and would be more comfortable texting. It's a free service to ANYONE!

This text crisis line works in all states in the continental United States. Anyone in a crisis can get a response by text.

I would love to hear from you about your goals, dreams, successes, and missteps. If you have questions along the way, I'd be happy to answer them to the best of my ability. If you feel so compelled, you may email me at **lksmith.author@gmail.com** or send me a handwritten note at L. K.Smith, PO Box 230, Elkhart, IL 62634. I am with you on this journey as you discover the great jewel that you are.

With warm hugs,
L. K. Smith

A NOTE TO PARENTS, GUARDIANS AND TEACHERS

Thank you for taking the time to read this guide. Parenting teens is hard! Like I tell the teens in my guide, if there is a word for *it*, someone before you has already *done it*. You can find all kinds of resources for fertility, pregnancy, infancy, the toddler years, etc. But a hands-on guide for teens? We're somewhat limited. Know that while I am walking with your teen on this journey, I am here for you, too. Sometimes just being able to hear that another parent has been in your shoes is enough.

As parents, the situations our kids face can feel devastating to us. We worry about how we will be judged by our peers, what the school will think, what the neighbors will think, what the family will say. Have you ever caught yourself saying to your child, "Don't you even care what people think about that?"

If your kids are like mine (and I suspect they are), they shrug their shoulders and say something like, "You really should stop caring about what other people think, Mom. It's the inside that counts. Isn't that what *you've* always said?"

So while this guide is designed for teens and young adults, there are valuable lessons in it for you, too. We need to learn to rise above what others think of us. We need to stop living vicariously through our children. We need to stop subscribing to the old-fashioned notion that our kids' letter grades, accolades, scholarships, leadership positions are a reflection of our great parenting. Because if that is true, the reverse is true: You are responsible for their failures, their missing assignments, their batting averages, their drug abuse, their teen pregnancies.

What?!? Yes. Do you get it now? Believing we are responsible for our kids' successes and failures is a set up. It gives us "false" power to make us feel like we've triumphed or we've failed as parents. Not true. While we certainly influence our children, they make their own decisions.

But our kids need help and guidance. They need love and support. They need to have their soul nurtured and respected. They make their own decisions, but we love them unconditionally when they make decisions we may not agree with. Or decisions that come with fallout.

When one of my own children went down a rough road, I learned some of the most valuable lessons ever. First, I quit caring about what other people thought of me, our situation, or my parenting. When people tried to engage in this type of "blamatory"(Yes, I made up that word!) conversation with me, I'd smile politely and change the subject. I also surrounded myself with good, true genuine people. No matter how close someone was to me previously, if they chose to engage in judgement or insensitivity, I moved on. I needed people who dared to hold me, wipe my tears, take me out for a coffee so I could gain some perspective. I needed friends who would say, " I have never been there, but I see your heart breaking. I am here." And then, they were.

I also realized over time, that the majority of the people either didn't know my situation, didn't care, or had moved on to the newest gossip. People talk about us much less than we think. When we feel like we are the topic of everyone's dinner conversation, that's our ego—our inner gremlin—telling us that our problems are bigger than they really are, that we are worthless, that no one else has such big problems. Choose your own gentle expletive here. Baloney! Hooey! Hogwash or Bull! I shut that ego down in many areas of my life. It no longer serves me, my husband, my children, my family, or my students.

Please try to remember that inside each child lives a unique spirit. Our goal in this life is to nurture that spirit, to let it grow and to let it thrive. Our hopes, dreams and aspirations for our children should come in the form of support for THEIR ideas, whether they choose to be artists instead of lawyers, animal welfare advocates instead of doctors. Truly, parents, it is not the end of the world if your otherwise responsible teen wants a body tattoo or piercing! When I hear someone say, "I just want better for my kids," ask yourself this: Are you pushing your agenda onto your children, trying to impose on them whatever you missed as a child? You longed for but never had piano lessons? It's not too late. Set a good example and take them now!

Then listen to your child. He or she will tell you what they like, want, hope and desire. Sometimes it's nonverbal. Do you remember how you learned your son didn't like peas? He left them on his plate time and time again. After twenty times, you thought to yourself, "Huh. I guess he doesn't like peas." It's the same process for our kids' activities. If they forget their piano music, are late to golf practice several times a month, if they forget their baseball glove at home six times in a row, when practice is an hour away, your child is trying to tell you something—most likely that this activity isn't for them. Be daring enough to have an open conversation where you really listen. All ears. Without your own agenda.

Tyler McNair is the son of the late Tennessee Titan football player Steve McNair. While approaching his senior year, Tyler's passion for dancing grew bigger than his passion for basketball. His basketball team on which he was the starting forward was poised to repeat the State Championship title. However, something inside of Tyler's spirit moved him to quit basketball and to give his full energies to dance. Unlike so many young people, he listened to his inner voice and he also had the full support of his mother, Mechelle. He was raised to honor his dreams, to nourish his spirit, and to be true to his passion. Tyler's story also has a lesson for parents: Our children will be truly, soulfully happy if we listen to them and help them to navigate— not *dictate*—their dreams. Despite the adversity his family faced, Tyler is an example of how being genuinely true to oneself will always bring success.

As parents we have an awe-inspiring role: to nurture the spirit inside each one of our children. Perhaps they will hurt less and feel more joy, if we are willing to listen with our hearts.

Warm regards,
L. K. Smith

HOW TO USE THIS GUIDE

From Disconnect to Reconnect: A 12-Week Guide to Offline Freedom and Joy for Teens and Young Adults

This guide will help you to look within your powerful self to find the answers to some of life's mysteries, to find inner strength and courage to change some harmful habits, so that you can find your amazing, authentic self already residing within.

Step by step, this guide will give you the power to celebrate small victories every day as you reclaim your true identity. You will reinvent yourself by moving toward your authentic self. Today, YOU get to decide how the world views you based upon your actions. When you complete this twelve-week guide, you will have unplugged from the technology around you and you will be in control. Does that mean you have to completely give up your phones and swear off social media? No. You don't. (You can breathe again now.) Like any area of your life that is off balance, you need to take a break. Hit "pause" from the craziness of technology, reflect on how it controlled you, and make adjustments.

In addition, I will give you the tools to define "you" according to your terms and not by who others say you are. My sincere hope is that when you complete this guide, you will care much less about what others think and a great deal more about honoring your true self and the gifts that lie within you. Ready to maximize your potential? Let's get started!

Each Chapter Can Stand Alone

I've written this guide so the chapters can stand alone. You can start and leave off where you like. If one chapter speaks to you more so than another, feel free to skip ahead. I know teens are busy and that you like to have an immediate solution. Please remember, though, that worthwhile change takes time. Time to reflect, to internalize, to practice. Allow yourself time to work through this process. To help with this process, I encourage you to dedicate a notebook or journal you can write in while going through this guide. Or if this is your guide, feel free to make notes in the margin. Work through each chapter, as each one is designed to help you to develop confidence, courage, a more positive self-image, good health and coping strategies. Throughout, the chapters offer simple, yet powerful affirmations, writing prompts, reflections and action steps. My hope for you once you complete this guide is that you greet each day feeling positive, fulfilled, goal-oriented and ready to make a difference.

CHAPTER ONE
Find Your Meaning in Life

You were born to make a positive difference in the world.

*Do you ever feel like something is off, but you can't quite put your finger on it? Do you feel like something is wrong with you, like you don't "measure up?" Do you question why you are here and your true purpose in life? Do you ever feel alone? Lonely? If you feel this way, you need to know that you are **never** really alone.*

Your morning alarm goes off—that annoying buzz in your ear signalling the start of another day. Another school day. You check your phone, and sure enough, it's time to get up. You throw your feet over the side of your bed and stumble to the shower. Maybe your thoughts turn to school, to a relationship, to the homework you should have done but didn't. Maybe you have a big quiz or test today. Doom! Why can't it just be Saturday already? Better yet, why isn't it summer? You feel stressed, depressed, disconnected and you've barely been awake for thirty minutes!

You feel pressure from everyone: teachers, parents, pastors, friends, jobs, yourself. Sound familiar? So much stress. (Very few teens have actually been taught how to deal with stress.) Don't you at times just want to tune it all out?

Or let me ask you this? What if you could wake up most days feeling excited about your day, energized about what is to come, happy knowing that you play an important, purposeful role in the lives around you?

Sound too good to be true? It isn't! David Whyte, English poet and philosopher said, "Genius is becoming something you were all along."[1] Whyte is right. You have the ability inside of you right now to awaken excited, energized and knowing you have purpose. You have the power to determine how happy you will be, what you will get done and how you can connect to the people who matter most in your life. Best of all, you have the power within you to learn how to love who you are today, despite any faults or flaws you may perceive. I know this, because I have worked with young adults and also taught high schoolers for 25 years, and I can say with total conviction that something beautifully universal is emitted from each one of you:

You love to be loved.

You love to learn.

You love to feel like you fit in somewhere.

But above all, you love to be seen. You want to know that someone sees you and the good you bring to the world. That's all any person really desires; to know we matter and that the world around us acknowledges our value.

How to Find Your Gift to the World
The Acorn Theory Says Each Individual is Born with a Gift or Form of Genius

In his bestseller *The Soul's Code*[2], author and psychologist James Hillman said that our calling in life is inborn, formed within us from birth, and that it's our mission in life to realize its imperatives. He called it the "acorn theory" — the idea that we are called into life with a uniqueness that asks to be lived. It is the idea that we each bring into the world a special gift. As we grow and mature, we come to recognize this gift.

What Have Others Told You? What Have They Repeatedly Said You Are So Good At?

Another way to recognize our special gift is to think back on what others who know us and are close to us have said we do so well.

PLUGGING IN PRACTICE:
Write in Your Journal

Identify what others repeatedly say is one of your gifts or your genius.

- Think of your interactions with closest friends, your parents or grandparents, your guardians, teachers, people you work or volunteer with.

- Recall situations where they have complimented you. What did you do that triggered the compliment?

- What did they each tell you? Where is the similarity or overlap in what they have said to you? Examples: "Wow! You really understand what I'm feeling." "You have such a beautiful way with words." "You solved that problem so quickly!" "You are so good with colors. I love how you decorated your room." "Your positive attitude gave me hope."

- Based on this exercise, have you gleaned any insights about what might be your innate gift or gifts? If so, what is this gift? Your unique genius?

Different Ways of Being Gifted—Howard Gardner's Multiple Intelligences

Harvard Professor of Education, Howard Gardner, proposed that the traditional notion of intelligence based solely on IQ is far too limiting. Schools focus on math, science and language skills. But Dr. Gardner says schools should place equal importance and attention on individuals who show gifts in the other intelligences: the artists, architects, musicians, naturalists, designers, dancers, therapists, entrepreneurs, and others who enrich the world in which we live.[3] His **Theory of Multiple Intelligences**[4] includes a broader range of intelligence which to date, include these:

- **Verbal-Linguistic intelligence** ("language and word smart")
- **Logical-Mathematical intelligence** ("number and reasoning smart")
- **Visual-Spatial intelligence** ("space, organizational, picture smart")
- **Bodily-Kinesthetic intelligence** ("coordination, strength, speed: body smart")
- **Musical intelligence** ("music appreciation or production smart")
- **Interpersonal intelligence** ("other people's moods, motivations and desires smart") Perhaps similar to EQ: emotional smarts
- **Intrapersonal intelligence** ("self-reflection, self-aware, inner feelings smart")
- **Naturalist intelligence** ("nature, environment smart")
- **Existential intelligence** ("deep questions smart")

Other Forms of Intelligence: Appreciative Intelligence

When you can rethink a situation, appreciate the positive, and see how our present choices and actions impact the future, you draw on *appreciative intelligence.* You see potential despite obstacles and challenges. This way of being smart is the subject of an article by by Tojo Thatchenkery and Carol Metzker.[5] The authors' research shows that "individuals with this ability show four consistent traits: persistence, conviction that one's actions matter, tolerance for uncertainty, and irrepressible resilience."

PLUGGING IN PRACTICE:
Write in Your Journal

The Earliest Memory You Have Of When Your Gift Came Into Play

Try to think back to your earliest memory of using your gift in some form. When you were a child, what did you love to do again and again? What did you do that put you into a flow state? In flow state, we block everything else out because we're in sync with our true passions. So what did you tend to do when you were in flow? Try to capture that past experience with as much detail as possible.

One Person Can Make a Difference

While your passions and talents will help you to make a big difference, you can also make a difference in people's lives by smaller gestures. In a journal or notebook, please list three examples in the past few weeks where you have had a positive impact on someone else.

- Did you smile at a lonely classmate?
- Hold the door for someone in a wheelchair?
- Offer to help out at home or at school?
- Spend an extra few minutes on the phone with a grandparent?

For each example, tell who you impacted. Also, what did you say or do? How did this make you feel? How do you think your words or deed made the other person feel?

CHAPTER TWO
Moving Through Sadness

Life is messy from time to time, but that doesn't mean we have to allow the messy parts to hold us captive.

If you are like most teens, you may feel anxious, sad, even worthless at times. Life hits you from all directions. You feel lost or stuck in a dark hole with no way out. Homework is piling up, your parents are on your case about cleaning your room, you get a text from a friend asking why you are being so distant. All you want to do is roll over in your bed and sleep.

Feeling Sad vs. Prolonged Sadness

Let's stop here for a moment to ask an essential question. If you cannot distinguish between normal teen sadness and true depression, and you feel great sadness or like engaging in self-harm, you could be in crises and need to seek immediate professional help.

No Shame in Seeking Help

You are not alone. In 2016, "An estimated 3.1 million adolescents aged 12 to 17 in the United States had at least one major depressive episode. This number represented 12.8% of the U.S. population aged 12 to 17."[6]

Like many teens, you may feel you have no one to talk to, or you feel embarrassed because to others, you look like the kid who has it all together. But you worry that if you get real and talk openly to someone, you will feel judged. You feel like your friends wouldn't really understand, so talking to them will make you feel even worse. Some of you may even feel guilty for feeling so bad! You may think, "I have a good home, my parents work hard, I have a car, a phone. I get good grades and I am involved in many school activities. I really shouldn't feel this way."

Does any of this sound familiar?

I am here to tell you that what you are experiencing is totally normal and you are NOT alone. In fact, ALL people experience these feelings to some degree at one point or another in their lives.

> **So before we go any further, know this:**
> 1. I hear you loud and clear.
> 2. I believe you.
> 3. Your feelings are real.
> 4. You can overcome these feelings.
>
> **And Remember This: You are Never Really Alone**

Sadness Can Be Beneficial

Did you know that the right amount of sadness might be helpful? In his article, "Four Ways Sadness May Be Good for You," psychology professor Joseph Forgas, says, "My research does suggest that mild, temporary states of sadness may actually be beneficial in handling various aspects of our lives."[7] Forgas says that sadness can act like a signal, prompting more effort and motivation when we feel challenged. We work hard to change our negative situation.

Prolonged Sadness is Not Beneficial

However, sadness is not always beneficial. Depression, a mood disorder defined, at least in part, by prolonged and intense periods of sadness—can be debilitating. This is the kind of sadness that requires professional help.

Alone vs. Lonely

Alone and lonely can mean so many different things. While we are never really alone, solitude can be a good thing, as it frees us to be who we truly are. Also, we benefit from having time alone to think, to recharge, to ponder some of life's beautiful mysteries. It also takes courage to make decisions alone. To reach deep inside and to say, "This is what my heart tells me is right."

The peaceful feeling we get from solitude is almost the opposite of feeling lonely. Loneliness comes from feeling no one is there for you or that you are somehow odd or different. Or separate. We are not separate. We are all connected on a Universal level to one another and to a Higher Power. It is true, however, that we might feel alone at times. Goethe, a German writer and scientist, said, "The soul that sees beauty may sometimes walk alone." As famous as he was, he could have been talking about himself. What's more, he said this in the 1700's and it is still true today! Those who see beauty see what is real rather than what is fake. It is not easy to embrace all that is real. For one, social media masks reality, entices us to create new identities for others to "like." And what's real about using software to look falsely thin or air-brushed? Our false online identities "mask" who we really are.

Sometimes those who know themselves well can feel lonely, because they are more evolved, ahead of the curve, more mature or insightful. They are smart enough and authentic enough to know they do not need to be part of the "in crowd." If you have ever read celebrity interviews, so many say they felt like outsiders growing up. Everybody feels like an outsider at some point in life. Teens included. The truth is, someone in your inner circle cares deeply. As part of this magnificent universe, you are never really alone.

Alone vs. Lonely: Consider & Write

Read the following examples and consider: Do you think the person in each example feels "alone" or "lonely?" After each, jot a few thoughts on the page here or in your journal.

1. When Tricia walks into the library at school, no one really looks her way. She usually sits alone in a one-person study carrel instead of at a group table. ____Alone ____Lonely Why do you think so?

2. You have known Jason for years. Since elementary school, he has wanted to be an astronaut. When others at school are having fun joking and talking, you usually see him curled up with a book about NASA. ____Alone ____Lonely Why do you think so?

3. On Sawyer's first day at his new school, he steps into the cafeteria and looks around for a place to sit. He sits at the first open seat he can find. ____Alone ____Lonely Why?

4. Mary is one of six children. When you walk past her house, you often see her sitting by herself on her porch swing. ____Alone ____Lonely Why do you think so?

5. Can you list three times during your week when you prefer to be alone?

The Power of Positivity

Sadness overcomes us when life gets overwhelming. When we feel overwhelmed, we magnify the negative in life and crowd out all of the good. It is no surprise that we become what we think about the most. Our thoughts have great power. On average, we each have 60,000 thoughts per day. Believe it or not, 80% of them—almost 50,000 of those thoughts—are negative! Why should we allow negative thoughts to consume our minds? If we think anger all the time, we will be angry. If we allow sadness to consume us, we will remain sad.

Why not develop a habit of positive thinking? Former football player Lewis Howes said, "I have learned that champions aren't just born; champions can be made when they embrace and commit to life-changing positive habits."[8] Howes pulled himself up from a miserable childhood to a life he now loves, because he gets to help others. Howes is also the host of "The School of Greatness" which is distributed as a podcast. He said, "I realized early on that when I commit to my vision and pursue it with 100% passion, anything is possible." He has a website called *About Lewis Howes*, if you'd like to read about his journey: https://lewishowes.com/about/

SO many times we get caught up in the garbage around us. It's too easy. Much like putting the wrong gasoline in a car, putting the wrong ideas and information into your head will produce a sluggish perspective. To share a bit of wisdom attributed to many individuals: we become what we pay attention to.

Makes perfect sense to me!

So set your attention on the pure, the whole, the genuine. Sometimes this takes getting out of our own minds because our perspective is tainted. Breathe deeply and ask for guidance on how to be positive. Getting yourself in the right frame of mind from the beginning of your day will work magic on your body. I tell myself, "Today is a great day...for a great day!" Do not settle for anything less than this. People are going to be crabby; don't let that stop you from your plan. It's too easy to get into a funk and not find your way back out. By starting your day happy, positive and in expectation of bliss... you will attract these into your life.

Positive self talk, also called positive affirmations, can help the most when you need to show up to life. Mornings, for example, when it's too easy to roll back over in bed and sleep. When your alarm goes off tomorrow, make a promise to yourself that you are going to get up and show up. Then greet the day with this affirmation, "With each new day, I get to start over."

Positive talk also helps when that feeling of sadness, or anxiety or confusion creeps in. If you are experiencing this sadness right now, tell yourself that this is the last day you are going to let your feelings get the better of you. When sad or negative thoughts creep in, about school or self-esteem or a social situation, meet these head on with affirmations such as, "I will do my personal best on today's exam," and "I am who I want to be starting this very minute," and "No one can make me feel bad without my consent."

Why wouldn't we want this mindset?! If we stay alone in our negative thoughts, they will surely get the better of us. You get to be in charge of what goes into your mind, and in this very moment, you will be positive, and you will step up and into your life. You can do it! And finally, when we repeat positive affirmations a few times in bed before we fall asleep each night, they work their way into our consciousness, relieving stress before sleep and offering a more peaceful wake-up call in the morning. Yes, life will be messy from time to time, but that doesn't mean we have to allow the messy parts to hold us captive.

PLUGGING IN PRACTICE:

Recall a time when you were genuinely happy. What did you see? What was happening around you? Transport your mind to that time and literally feel how the peace will come over you. Having control over your mind will give you the edge you need to succeed. Make a decision from the get go. You decide to have a good day. No matter what stands in your path, you tell yourself: "This is an obstacle Linda warned me about. It will not beat me down, nor will it stand in my way. I will breathe through this and I will come out ahead."

Positivity attracts positivity. What you think about, you will bring about. If you think you are beaten, unlikeable and depressed, guess what? You are. Now turn this thought process around. Think of yourself as kind, loving, helpful and blessed... and you will be! If you look at what all the great minds in this world have in common, it is the simple fact that *they believed they could,* so they did. Your birthright is to be successful and to follow your passion. Remember, if what you are doing is for good, you will leave your mark on this world. You cannot go wrong when you have a positive, happy, pure, clean mind. Rise above the idle gossip; rise above the news that wants to make you depressed; rise above the people who say you can't do this or you can't do that. Yes, you can and you will. Set your intention to be great!

Plugging Back In: Seven Exercises for Daily Practice:

1. Tapping Into Feelings—Guided Visualization

    a. Be still. Set an alarm for five minutes and trust that it will go off. Then, forget about the alarm. Closing your eyes, turn inward and listen to your mind. What is it telling you? Breathe deeply and fully. What does your heart hear? Sit and be still as you continue to focus on your breath. Push any "real time" thoughts out of your mind and listen to the voice that may sound unfamiliar to you. The one telling you that you are already enough. The one inviting you to share your gifts with the world. The one bringing peace and optimism and joy. We will tap into these feelings often. We will call these your "core feelings."

    b. Once the alarm sounds, write down the words you've heard. Did you hear any goals mentioned? If so, jot them down. What three words describe your core feelings? Jot those down, too.

    c. Put these core feelings on a sticky note and keep them handy. Place them on your mirror in your room, your locker, your favorite book, inside your lunch bag. You need to remind yourself every day how you can tap into these feelings to rekindle the happiness and joy in YOUR self that YOU created.

2. No-Phone Challenge: Turn your phone off for fifteen minutes. During that fifteen minutes, walk, do sit ups, do a plank, stretch, sit in downward dog- or do a combination of these movements. Do something physical! Focus your thoughts on your body, your mind and your spirit. Be aware and conscious of what your body is capable of doing. After the fifteen minutes are up, breathe deeply five times. Ask yourself the following questions: Did I miss anything? Are the alerts on my phone more important than my core feelings? Am I making myself a priority? You may be surprised that time passed more quickly than you imagined. Perhaps it was really tough for you. That's okay. We're building self awareness. This is a journey, not an ending.

3. **Small Gesture Olympics.** Today's practice is an all day event. Do small, simple gestures for those around you. These may include holding the door for someone, smiling in the halls at school, telling your teacher "thank you" as you walk out of class, making a connection with a classmate, doing a small task at home without being asked or told. Keep track in your journal every time you create a small gesture for someone. At the end of the day, replay the moments in your mind and take note of how you felt each time. Add these feelings to your core list!

4. **Mood Check-In.** How was your mood today? Was there a time when you started to feel crummy, put yourself back on track, and reached out and did something kind for someone else? Consider this a HUGE victory.

5. **Water Challenge:** Commit to drinking water all day. No soda, no sports drinks, no coffee, no energy drinks. Pure water. How many ounces did you consume? Now compare that number to yesterday. Is it higher? Then, you are on the right track! If it's lower, be vigilant as to how you feel. If you had a soda, did it make you feel sluggish? Don't beat yourself up over it. Look at the times you treated your body kindly. Again, this is not a contest. You are working to be more self-aware.

6. Pick a Topic. Today's challenge is to pick anything you've ever wondered about- or maybe you haven't! Open up a window and type in something you've wanted to learn about. It can be something huge like how bees know when to pollinate a flower, or something as simple as the looking up the world's population. The idea is to stimulate your mind to think about something new. Or you might want to think of something familiar in a new way! All of those plastic containers we recycle...what ELSE can we make out of them? This new thinking might open an area for you to pursue later in life. Now, take that information and think about it. What surprised you?

7. Highs. Sighs. Oh Mys! At the end of the day, do some quiet reflection. If your journal is handy, you may choose to write this down. However, if you are tired, mulling this over in your mind works, too. What was the high of your day? Was there something spectacular? Remember, you define spectacular; no one else. Spectacular to someone else does not mean the same to you. This is not about judgment. Let's be real; we all have bad times. So what was a sigh today? A ho hum moment. Not do as well as projected on a quiz? Sigh. Not get the job you applied for? Sigh. Acknowledge the sigh, but move on. "Oh my!" refers to those moments that take you aback. A glorious sunset. An amazingly clear night where the stars bounce and leap. A puppy hops up and licks your cheek. Recognizing and honoring ALL parts of your day gives you balance in your world. You realize life happens, but it doesn't have to stop you in your tracks.

Stop looking outside of yourself for validation. Does the world change? Is it fluid? Of course it is. We know the world is always moving and always in a state of change. So, too, are people. When we allow others to define who we are, we are putting our trust into something which is in a constant state of change.

Think of this scenario: You want to wear a new outfit to the movies, but you just aren't sure. What do you do? Do you text your friends and ask what they are wearing? Do you change your outfit several times? Look within. You have everything you need to make this decision.

You have purpose. You have worth. You are enough. You matter and your life matters.

PLUGGING IN PRACTICE:
Guided Affirmations

Talking to yourself in a kind, gentle way is the first step in achieving this new level of happiness and freedom.

Turn to the Affirmations Page. Close your eyes and take a deep breath. Open your eyes, and run your finger over the list, and when you are comfortable, stop. Look down and read what is there. Make this your affirmation for the day. Write it on a sticky note or note card, and keep it close. When you start to hear or feel that negative inner voice, revert back to this positive note. Read it over and over. This new habit takes practice. These new messages take some getting used to. And it might take more than one day of reading a sticky note to reprogram your mindset. If it were that simple, we'd have sticky notes posted all over the world, and the whole world would be one joyful group of people. But what you *are* doing is taking the first step to inviting the real you to surface. You are making the effort. Remember that what we put in is what we put out. We have to plug into the positive around us even when we don't feel like it. We are "talking" this walk together, allowing the real you to surface, the happier you who feels purpose and a sense of worth. Talking to yourself in a kind, gentle way is the first step in achieving this new level of happiness and freedom.

For more on positive affirmations, read *37 Affirmations for Teens*, on this website: **http://7mindsets.com/affirmations-for-teens/**

AFFIRMATIONS PAGE:

I am utterly beautiful.

I am created in the image of the Divine.

I am enough.

I am worthwhile.

I have value.

I have a purpose.

I am here to do good in this world.

I have a brilliant mind.

I am full of light and goodness.

I am on my path to greatness.

I am surrounded by those who love me.

I am a good friend.

I am a creature with a Divine purpose.

I am never alone.

I am a person of peace.

I am filled with good intentions.

I will use my life for a higher purpose.

I will surround myself with happy, joyful people.

I am worth all that is good in this world.

I am smart and I will tap into my intelligence today.

I can solve problems.

I can be a good listener.

I can seek the best in others.

I am full of talent.

I am mentally strong.

I have the ability to do what is right and just.

I can live out my full potential.

I can remember to be motivated today.

I will drink plenty of water today to keep my brain fresh.

I have the ability to make good choices.

I am full of joy today.

I can forgive others.

I can focus on the good.

I am capable of using my talents.

I will plug into life today, and I will be present to those around me.

I will smile whenever I make eye contact with another person.

I accept myself for who I am today and where I am today.

I have unlocked potential inside of me.

I am a good friend.

I have solid boundaries, and I know how to respect them.

I am a work in progress.

I love myself- all of myself.

I am loved by many people in my life—some I know;
    some I have yet to meet.

CHAPTER THREE
Healthy Alternatives to
Stuffing, Alcohol and Drugs

You are filled with goodness and light. And today is the
day you are after. If you can tell yourself that what happened yesterday,
last week, last year is in the past and that is where it shall remain,
you are one step ahead.

This will be one of the longest chapters in this guide because there is so much to say on these topics: alcohol, drugs, mobile device addiction, consequences, forgiveness. Blocking your emotions, or "stuffing" as I like it call it, is really harmful to your body for so many reasons. When teens cram or force or "stuff" what they are genuinely feeling, the result can be so detrimental. In this chapter, the main points are to help you to understand the influences that lead you to harmful habits and actions, to be truthful about consequences, to find a way out by seeking the help of a professional or trusted adult; and finally, to see that you can be more, achieve more and feel more by looking inward to find the real you—and your life purpose. Today is the day for new starts!

Alcohol and Drug Abuse: Behind the Scenes
Our youth today is in crisis. Absences from school, drug and alcohol use, cutting, process addiction, disordered eating and depression are at an all-time high. Research has indicated that at least one in five teens suffer from anxiety or depression. The National Institute of Mental Health 2016 report states: "An estimated 3.1 million adolescents

aged 12 to 17 in the United States had at least one major depressive episode. This number represented 12.8% of the U.S. population aged 12 to 17. The study also showed that 60% of these teens received no treatment for their depression.[9]

A shocking statistic. Untreated, depression can lead to significant emotional, functional, and physical problems.

Remember in grade school how Red Ribbon Week was fun? You would learn some statistics about drugs and drinking and how harmful they were to your body. You lived for theme days: "Dress in All Red," "Put a Cap on Drugs," or "Be a Superhero!" Perhaps your school even had a speaker come in and talk to you in a motivational way about the dangers he or she faced and how their life is dramatically different today as a result. Red Ribbon Week encourages kids to make smart choices. But what may work for 8-12 year olds is not effective for teens. If a high school has any kind of smart-choices program, it needs to be as hard hitting as the industry influencing the teens. In addition, our high school curriculums are so packed that few high schools participate in Red Ribbon Week.

As a culture, we are bombarded with drugs and alcohol. Advertisers make millions of dollars a year to glamourize the industry. Beer commercials show everyone having a great time, partying, laughing, getting along, and all the while being fashionable and supremely good looking. How do we combat the impact of this industry on adolescents? We cannot just slap a red ribbon on our shirts and think we are winning the race. And as for those parties...

If you've ever been to a party, think back to what it looked like in comparison. My guess is it looked something more like this: Somebody either stole the alcohol, had an adult commit a crime and buy the alcohol for underage drinkers, or had a parent (who was trying to be the neighborhood *buddy*) secure the alcohol and willingly permit the party. Perhaps it was a combination of the aforementioned. So before the party gets into full swing, several people already feel guilty for doing something illegal. After a few hours, people are drunk, their liquid courage in full throttle. Someone is throwing up. A couple throws angry words and insults to one another. Gossip starts. People judge. Someone is trying to convince her friends that she is "fine" and can drive. Drama, tears and anger spew. I could stop here, but chances are there's more: jealousy, a fist fight, best friends arguing, then throw in some pills from the medicine cabinet in the master bedroom and you have a real gig going on! The smell of pot wafts through the air and people you thought were on the cross country team are vaping off in the corner, *because, you know, it's safe- not like real cigarettes.* But that's not all! Either curfew is looming, the cops have been called, or your ride is leaving and it's time to head home. Or maybe you'll head over to a friend's house because her mom doesn't care if you party. Then the lies start in answer to

Where were you?

Who were you with?

What were you doing?

Why are you so late getting home?

Regret rolls in the very next day. First with the post-party hangover. Head still spinning. Then Xanax, the post-party cure that your friend's college-aged sister surprised her with. Then the nightmares unfold. Why did you do that? Why did you say that? You check your phone and scroll through your texts, your Snapchat, your Instagram. The feeling of dread comes over you. Guilt and shame sink deep into your belly. You do not recall taking that photo. That's not who you are. Maybe if you just go to sleep for a few more hours, it won't be so bad. Maybe the pressure will be off of you and the drama will have shifted to someone else.

But it always looks so glamorous in the movies and in the commercials. Whatever happened to the pure bliss and happiness... as promised? Sadly, you've been lied to. Advertisers have a product to sell.

Allow me a brief story. A friend once took a boat trip from the coast of Key West to the Dry Tortugas. During the first hour, the water was calm and everyone sipped lemonade, laughed and snapped photos and had a great time. A young couple owned the boat and served as captain and first mate. Soon after the boat took off, my friend said to the first mate, "This is so calm and nice. What a lovely morning to sail!" The first mate looked at her husband, then back at my friend. "Yes," she said. "These trips always start like this. Just wait." About thirty minutes later, my friend caught her drift. She told me that most passengers looked like a makeup artist had blue-tinted their faces. Hunched over, seasick, they all held their stomachs. Some lay with their heads on the dinette tables, lifting them long enough to eject breakfast. "We paid good money for our tickets," she said. "We expected a great time and a beautiful journey. We did not expect big waves."

The ups and downs of her experience reminded me of the parties teens attend. What begins as "fun," can turn sour by night's end. Now multiply this party scenario times ten. Can you see how the cycle of party after party compounds problems? Stop and think about the last time you turned to drugs or alcohol. What were the outcomes? Did you feel happy, uplifted and positive about yourself? Maybe you got lucky that once. Minimal collateral damage. Chances are, though, something shameful resulted. Now take a deep breath as I offer perspective. The good news is you don't have to live in *that* moment forever. That was yesterday. Or last week. Or last month. This is today. Here and now. And you are human and you will make mistakes. Using drugs and alcohol is a mistake, but you can learn to forgive yourself and move forward. You are not the sum of your mistakes. You are so much more than that. Today is the day you are after. If you can tell yourself that what happened yesterday, last week, last year is in the past and that is where it shall remain, you are one step ahead. Be in today. Be in the moment. Slow down and recognize today as a clean start, a fresh slate, a new time to create for yourself, to ensure a better tomorrow.

One of my favorite quotes from Buddha is as follows: "The secret for both mind and body is not to mourn for the past, worry about the future, or anticipate troubles...but to live in the present moment wisely and earnestly." When it comes to drugs and alcohol, living wisely might mean seeking professional help for treatment or intervention.

Mobile Device Addiction: My Personal Struggle

Another area of huge concern is that of process addiction, or compulsively using your device. You can't put it down. Relatively new to the scene, process addiction can affect anyone, anytime, including *Yours Truly*. When I read the statistic that teens were spending on average 5-7 hours per day on their phones, at first I thought, "No Way! That's too high!" But then I got honest with my own usage and found I was spending roughly 7 hours a day online myself. My gut reaction? I quit all social media and the games I had downloaded on my phone. I tend to do that: I think in terms of black and white: all or nothing. Good or evil. Right or wrong. So instead of finding balance, I gave it up altogether.

After I gave myself some time to process (See what I did here?), I realized I had some guilt and shame to work through. I felt guilty because I knew in my heart of hearts that sitting on the corner of my couch cozied up next to my sons did not equal quality time. Not even by my own definition. And as a teacher, I'm well aware of the mental health consequences of too much technology. So why did it take me so long to see what was really happening?

Picture the four of us sitting in the living room together, but instead of connecting to one another, we are each absorbed in our own hand-held devices. At first glance, not a problem, right? I mean our evenings are pretty chill; no one is mad, and occasionally someone will pop up and share a funny story or an interesting video they came across. Don't get me wrong. My kids also participate in travel sports, school sports and church. We even have device-free dinners! But that day on the couch, I realized that we were all just a heartbeat away from mobile device addiction.

This was *not* the kind of togetherness I want for my family. This was *not* how I want my kids to remember their childhoods. I knew that to find true connection and deep communication, I needed to lead by example.

So, I decided to fight back. This was undoubtedly one of the hardest things I have had to do. I had to first look at my behavior which had spun out of control. What was this behavior exactly? I wasn't a 5-a-day poster on Facebook. I might only tweet once a week or occasionally post a cool pic on Instagram. So it wasn't the over documentation of my life that was concerning. The problem was my constant, excessive liking of other people's statuses and my going overboard with the number of comments to build them up. I know this doesn't sound bad; but I had to look at my motivation. I wasn't liking or making a nice comment just for kicks. I was doing it for approval. I wanted to make a smart comment and have someone agree with me. I thought that telling someone, "You are beautiful no matter what," would win me points in the social media realm. Instead of being motivated by genuine love and concern, it was my ego building up another's ego. This is unfair to me to seek outside approval, and it is unfair to the people on whose posts I am commenting or liking. I was seeking validation from the outside. As if to say, "Look at me! *See? I am a good person; I made a nice comment.*" This is *not* an authentic way to live.

The realization of what I was doing really upset me. So I quit. I made a decision to delete the apps from my phone and to swear off social media. I had to ask myself some deep questions, such as "What higher purpose is social media serving me in my life?" I didn't have a good answer. I just didn't. I ask you the same:

- What higher purpose is social media serving in *your* life?
- When you post to Snapchat, what happens? Do you feel good?
- How is social media putting value into your life or into the lives of others?

Maybe you are different from me. Maybe you are running a nonprofit that helps small children across the globe, so your use of social media is to connect to donors who are supporting your cause. This is tremendous if this is your story. This was not, however, my story.

I have to be honest—the notion of quitting social media initially scared me. I told a few trusted friends and, of course, I disclosed my plan to my family, so I would automatically be held accountable. My kids keep me honest. They are my cheerleaders in life and want to see me be honest, so they know they have a footprint to follow if they so choose.

Their reactions were mixed. My husband was relieved; he felt I was spending way too time online. Sometimes, I was so absorbed online, I didn't hear him tell me this. Other times, I just ignored him. I justified this excess use. "I need some down time," I'd say. "I need to decompress. I've been thinking all day!" Excuses. Excuses. Not OK. My sons were a little freaked out, because they know that when *I* change, *they* change! What did this mean to their freedom? My daughters were open and understood where I was coming from. They, too, have taken breaks, realizing how toxic it is to be caught in the trap of social media envy and online comparison.

I have to say, after the initial few days offline, I was so much happier. I had time to get little things done, things I had put off. I could take walks, write this book, be emotionally available to my children. It was hard, but the payoff is completely worth it. Three months later, I have no regrets. What's more, my life is fuller. And yes, I am keeping it "real."

As a result of how good I was feeling, I felt it was time to ask the experts: My teenage students. I took an unofficial survey and asked them, "If you had to give up social media immediately, but none of your friends did, how would you feel?" Some of their responses: Disconnected, forgotten, bored, horrible, lonely, life over, devastated, sad, empty, alone, left, behind, friendless, outdated, stranded, distressed, confused, mad, lost, missing out. Only two students said it wouldn't be too bad. In fact, one mentioned the simple thought of giving up social media felt like a gift. "When I imagined being off social media, I felt free. I felt I would have more time to finish important things." Do any of those comments sound familiar? So... too much social media is harmful to our mental health. But swearing off social media is downright nerve wracking and stressful! This tells me that our culture invests so much time in technology that we are forgetting the joy of living in real time as real people.

Another component of social media is how it owns you. Quite literally. It hijacks our brains...the part of our body that controls functions such as breathing, eye movements, blood pressure, heartbeat and swallowing! Are you going to stand for that?!

I was not in control of my own mind because -and it's no secret- social media deliberately creates rewards that trigger a dopamine release—a pleasure chemical in your brain. The more you *like, scroll, or interact*, the higher the level of dopamine released in your brain- keeping you addicted.[10] This is all happening behind the scenes. People we do not know control our obsessions, behavior and body chemistry. You'll see more on this in Chapter Seven.

What can we do about this? We should be shouting these truths from our rooftops. Civil disobedience. We should be Social Media Mavericks, Truth Activists. At the very least, we MUST be smart consumers, in charge of our own behavior. Otherwise, how do I know I am on the right path? We are not as a culture going to relinquish our rights to free thinking, free living and free thoughts. We ARE responsible for our behavior because it is our duty to know what we are subjecting our brains to. It's no different than the food and drink choices we make. If it isn't a healthy food, why are we eating it?

New Habits, New Actions, Better Outcome When You Can Get to the Root of Your Pain

So then, what do we do? Well, we start by looking at the WHY. Why do teens drink, drug, vape, cut, view porn, and make other decisions that negatively impact their lives? Because they hurt. Teens hurt in lots of ways. Sometimes the issues are deep-rooted and serious like abuse or neglect. In such cases, these principles here will still apply and are still super useful; however, as I say from the start of this book, I am not a psychologist, psychotherapist nor M.D., nor can I replace one, so if you are dealing with an ongoing problem or ongoing sadness or depression, SEEK IMMEDIATE HELP

- from a trusted adult
- Text 741741 from anywhere in the USA to text with a trained Crisis Counselor
- or call the National Suicide Prevention Lifeline: 1-800-273-TALK (8255)

But it is still important for you to know that you are not alone, you do have worth and you do matter. If you or a friend need help, please seek professional help immediately. Being able to ask for outside, professional help is pretty scary. Not many people want to admit they have a problem, but we are human and we ALL have problems to some degree or another. I know how tough it can be to reach out to another person and say, "It's too much. I need help here." Our goofy pride gets in the way. We fool ourselves into thinking, "I am the only one who feels this way. I am the only one going through this. No one else will ever understand." Recognize the voice of your inner critic and banish it from the conversation! I strongly encourage you to reach out to someone—a teacher, a friend, a friend's parent, a pastor, a school guidance counselor, a neighbor you trust. Anyone who can help you to connect with a trusted adult is a good starting point.

On other occasions, however, sometimes teens just hurt and they don't know why. They feel moody or sad or insignificant. They try so hard to put up a false front, to mask their true emotions, by wearing that forced smile. Inside, though, they don't feel alive. The only solution is to get to the root of your pain.

We Follow The Crowd To Feel Accepted

Another reason so many teenagers are on social media is for validation. You want to fit in, and feel loved and accepted. So you look at other people and size them up. Are they popular? If so, what are they doing? Are they posting nude pics because it's a way to get attention? Are they sexting with other teens because it's the next best thing? Because it's risky? It's fun? Teens are being made to feel that the more outrageous their behavior is, the more people will follow them, and like them, thereby propelling them to popularity or acceptance. But the question is, who are you when you put your head down at night?

What purpose are you serving? Whose purpose are you serving? *Ah, no regrets though*, you think. *We are young. We are just living. It's old-fashioned thinking that everyone is a virgin. It's harmless.*

I totally disagree. It's not harmless. Harmless means no one gets hurt. Is that true? Maybe no one else is getting hurt. But YOU are somebody else. What harm is coming to you as a result of your behaviors?

Without social media, how else are you supposed to know what's going on with your friends? How do you stay in the know and connected to your peers? Feel like you fit in? If you swear off all technology, you will be alone. And no one wants to be alone. Besides, being all alone for a length of time it isn't the healthiest route. We were created to be social. But not at all costs.

Smartphones and Internet—When Benefits Morph into Addictions

"The brains of Internet addicts may undergo chemical changes similar to those of alcoholics and other drug addicts, according to a new study."[11] Some parents are shocked when they find out their kids have been up all night texting, tweeting, posting, snapping. Apps, games, social media, etc. They believed that when their child went to bed, they may have texted for a few minutes. However, the truth is many teens are on their phones all night. Some of you may fall into the category of sleeping for a few hours, getting up, checking your phone, responding, dozing off again only to repeat this process night after night, all night long. You aren't giving your body the chance to rest. I am not judging you; I am helping you to see that some behaviors can be changed to give you immediate results. Remember part of this journey is to continue to ask yourself, how is my behavior serving me to reach my higher purpose? Being sleep-deprived is not the answer.

PLUGGING IN PRACTICE:

- Recall: When was the last time you engaged in a "stuffing" behavior. Remember, this is the word I use to convey what teens do when they "cram" or "force" (or "stuff") their true feelings deep inside. What did you feel prior to hiding your emotions? Were you aware that what you were doing was hurtful to yourself? What did you expect to happen? Did you feel better about who you are and who you want to become the day after?

- Process: Take a minute or two to breathe deeply. Slow your heart down. Ask yourself what you would do differently, given the chance.

- Forgive yourself. Say in your mind the following: I forgive myself for my behavior. I will not carry this with me through the day. I will start fresh, I will have gentle thoughts, and I will do something kind for myself. The kindness can include eating something healthy, drinking more water, going for a run, doing yoga, or journaling. I will also do something kind for someone else.

- Throwing shade is the expression teens use to speak ill of a friend or acquaintance to denounce or to disrespect them; it's also referred to as trash talk. The act of doing so often gets laughs or validation. But when you "throw shade" or act rude, you are really showing insecurity and weakness. Being kind shows positive self-esteem and strength. So, instead of throwing shade, I challenge you to throw sunshine! Speak well of others. Be the one to throw kindness, care and concern. Turn it around and live YOUR best life.

Tech Use Self-Study—Become More Aware!

So what you can do? You can start by being aware. Simply knowing how long you are on your device is helpful. Before you actually log any amount of time in the chart below, take a guess as to how much time you think you're spending online, texting, snapping, posting, scrolling, etc. Then, I want to you to fill in the chart for three days. Be honest. No one is seeing this but you. Afterwards, tally your minutes and hours and compare to what you originally thought prior to the exercise. What did you find? Are you surprised?

If you were spot on and it exceeds the recommended daily allowance, can you cut back? Even cutting out 30 minutes a day will equate to 182.5 hours per year or the equivalent of 7.6 days annually. You will gain back an ENTIRE week of your life. That's pretty astounding.

What if your results were much, much more than you anticipated? What can you do about it?

Practice the same principle. Start slowly by cutting back.

Technology Usage

	Instagram	Snapchat	Tumblr	Twitter	Texting	Misc.
Day 1						
Day 2						
Day 3						

How many hours do I think I am on my phone/device per day?

_____

According to my chart, how many hours per day am I actually spending on my phone/device? _____

An Invitation to Break the Cycle!

So what did you learn? The chronic texters, posters, scrollers need to do the obvious thing: Ask for help. Have a talk with a trusted adult and voice your concerns. Explain that while you may not be ready to go cold-turkey, you do realize you are ready for a change and need some help. Try to commit to at the very least giving yourself the gift of sleep. Ask the adult (go ahead, password protect and lock it down; heck just shut it off!) if he would be willing to take your phone from you each night at an agreed upon time. I would suggest somewhere in the neighborhood of 10:00 p.m. You need a good 30 minutes to unwind away from the blue screen or the light emitted from the device. That gives you the opportunity to clear your mind and have some down time before going to sleep. Commit to handing it over at the agreed upon time. You should also determine when you get it back in the morning. Probably try to get up, shower, and eat before doing so. This will do a few things: It will get you moving faster as you have an incentive, and it will give you time to consider your goals and plans for the day without interruption. Trust me. After a few nights of developing this new routine, you should feel better. As South Australian sleep researcher Dr Sarah Blunden puts it: "Sleep is the foundation of all physical and mental health essentially. That sounds very radical but it's true."[12] I've never heard anyone complain about feeling worse after a solid night's sleep!

CHAPTER FOUR
Move It, Shake It,
for Optimal Well-Being

"While I dance I cannot judge, I cannot hate, I cannot separate myself from life. I can only be joyful and whole. This is why I dance."
—*Hans Bos*[13]

Picture this: The sun creeps through her bedroom window, gently hitting her face. She stretches long and gently, takes in a few deep, meaningful breaths, throws back the covers and hops out of bed. Her mind focusing on what a great day it is for a great day. Glancing at her Apple watch, she notes the time: 5:45 am. Perfect. She puts on her comfy clothes, laces up her worn but sturdy running shoes, and water bottle in hand, heads out the door for a swift jog. Why? She realized how good fitness energized her and elevated her mood!

Across town, in similar fashion, he, too, in his workout clothes stands at the kitchen counter, takes his vitamins and drinks his protein shake. He heads to his basement and notes on his calendar that it is strength training day. With confidence, he cranks up the volume on his headphones and jumps in. Slow, steady reps as he realizes just how far he's come in such a short time. Why? He decided to make fitness a part of his path to greatness.

You can commit to the same, and this could be YOU!

I'm Not an Athlete, What do I do?
When I suggest an active lifestyle program to someone, I often hear, "But I am not athletic." And I can sense that person's brain

default to a feeling of dread, with visions of unflattering workout clothes and punishing exercise regimes. Well, I have good news! We are not training for a marathon! I'm not talking gym membership nor personal trainer (unless you so choose). This is not a weight loss program. If you happen to drop body fat as a result of increased physical activity, bonus! We are simply commiting to about an hour and a half of physical activity per week. Thirty minutes times three. Or four twenty-minute periods. Or six fifteen-minute periods. I know you get it. Or as the character Proctor said in the poorly rated movie, *R.I.P.D.*..."I think you're smelling what I'm selling."

Your goal is to work toward optimal well-being by nurturing body, mind, and spirit. This is what it truly means to be in good health. If you have any concerns about any of the activities in this chapter, consult your physician.

Reframe Your Sense of What it Means to Workout

The word origin of "workout" dates back to the mid 14th century and essentially means "the condition of being in active operation." Think about it. Nothing in this definition has anything to do with the *coulds*, *shoulds*, and *woulds*. Much like we reframe the word "Failure" in Chapter Five let's reframe the meaning of "work out." To work out is to be active. Forget "Shoulda, coulda, woulda." No dwelling on the past. Start fresh today! After all, this guide is about starting over. Second chances. Practice *not* perfection. I love that. Reframe your mind and you reframe your future.

What it Means to Workout: From Walking to Alligator Wrestling

Just kidding about the alligators, but you do get to choose your activity. If you can't do yoga, go for a walk. If you don't like walking, get on your bicycle or get on the floor for gentle stretching. Use your doorway for resistance workouts and toning. Lift canned soup or beans if you do not have dumbbells. My friend has a plaque that reads: *We Dance in This Kitchen*. If you do not like to dance, skip rope or walk your dog more often! The end of this chapter offers more options.

Move Your Body; Still Your Mind

An active lifestyle program is about being kind to your body and releasing endorphins which will bolster your mood naturally. By getting your heart rate elevated, you will release stress, anxiety and pressure from your everyday life. Being active cleanses negative energy from your body in a natural way, and leaves you with a healthy glow.

Commit to Realistic Goals...AND Write Them Down!

Research indicates that when you write down a goal, you are more than likely to achieve this goal than if you just state it in your head. So plan ahead.

Decide from this day forward, that you are going to take care of your body in the physical sense. Tell yourself that you are worth the little practice that this will entail and know that in doing so, you will improve so many of your body's functions. Begin by setting your intention. Then put it in writing. For instance, you might state, "Beginning today, I intend to get some form of physical exercise three times a week for 30 minutes. I am going to be kind to my body. I know that I have the option of increasing this activity, but to begin, I am willing to commit to three times a week."

All you need is an action plan and the desire to commit. On your calendar, find three days and times that will work in your schedule. Now, mark them on your calendar, and when the time comes, show up! And have fun figuring this out! Treat it like a gift to yourself, because optimal well-being is a gift. In fact, it's the crown jewel.

Where to Find Movement Programs - There's an App for That

There are literally thousands of free programs online for any lifestyle. *Couch to 5k* is a popular app and it gets you pointed in the right direction with a plan on how to activate yourself.

Mother Nature is Free

For so many teens, money is an issue. Gym memberships can be expensive and then you feel obligated to go. This adds unwanted stress. This is not what you've signed up for. Instead, head outdoors! Mother Nature does not charge for walks, skips, or runs.

Music

You can find free dance music anywhere. Pop some good dance tunes on and get your own private dance party going! The old quote, "Dance like no one is watching" applies here.

Old School PE

I have friends who are old enough to remember how President Kennedy's administration developed and promoted a school curriculum to improve physical fitness for school children nationwide. The motto of the program was "Fitness Program for All That Takes Only a Few Minutes a Day." Think of the old movies you've seen where kids are doing sit ups, crunches, push ups, planks and wall squats. Yep! Basically, that was the program! You can do three sets of ten just about anywhere, in very little time, and again, for free!

Enlist a Buddy

Find a friend or family member and see if he or she would be willing to go run around a local playground with you. Doing the monkey bars can torch some serious calories!

Dog Walking

Ask a friend or neighbor if their dog needs to be walked. This is an excellent way to get your thirty minutes of exercise in; you might be earning money while doing so; and you get to bond with a furry creature. Win-win! Boom!

Laughter Yoga

Yes, it is a laughing workout that offers body-mind wellness! Don't laugh! Oh, I mean, go ahead and laugh. I know it's a funny exercise concept, but it's an amazing workout, if you call laughing a workout. And it is! Dr. Madan Kataria (now known as the Laughter Guru) started Laughter Yoga.[14] It is a real exercise program with trained teachers! It offers the same relaxation and cardiovascular benefits as other workouts! And it offers the same deep-breathing detox benefits one gains from other forms of yoga. An Oxford University study suggested that the endorphin effect of Laughter Yoga helped people with their chronic pain.[15] You can find laughter yoga exercises on Youtube, in audio form or in real classes offered at some gyms. You can learn more about Laughter Yoga, on Dr. Kataria's official website: https://laughteryoga.org/

Zumba

Zumba is a fitness program that combines Latin and international music with dance moves. Zumba cds can offer a fun, upbeat way to get your heart rate up. The dance moves are easy to master with a little practice, but even if you don't get all of them down, the goal is to move to the beat! Let the music guide you along as you *move* closer to the optimal you.

Strength Bands for Mobility and Resistance Training

Strength bands are a quick, easy way to build muscle tone and increase flexibility without the expense of a full blown weight set. Plus, they fit anywhere so you don't have to be concerned about missing a workout because your parents *insist* you go to that family reunion five hours away.

Your Post Workout High

The important part is not what you are doing, but rather that you are getting out and being active. It's so important to your state of mind, focus and well being.

A 2015 study by a Stanford University research group[16] showed that a 90-minute walk in nature helped healthy participants break the cycle of negative thinking, a cycle that worsens depression. This same research group found that deliberately focusing on a task can also deactivate the cycle of negative thinking. As Melanie Greenberg writes in Psychology Today, "It doesn't matter whether it's tidying your closets, doing the laundry, or doing a crossword puzzle, getting an 'on-task' focus can deactivate the negative-thinking cycle and instead activate the 'on-task' areas of the brain."[17]

When you exercise, your body releases chemicals called endorphins. Endorphins interact with the receptors in your brain that reduce your perception of pain. Endorphins also reduce our stress, and trigger a positive feeling in the body. That's why we call them "happy." Releasing your happy endorphins will get you into a positive state of mind, and you'll feel better about yourself as you continue on your road to greatness.

PLUGGING IN PRACTICE

- Make your fitness goals come to fruition by writing them down. Using the weekly planner at the end of this chapter, fill in the obligations you have for the week. Include school, work, doctor appointments, club meetings, etc. Find a space where you can plug in 30 minutes three times a week. Make a commitment to yourself to engage in one of the activities suggested above, or be daring enough to come up with your own. It doesn't matter; the point is, you get moving and you commit. Add these dates in your day planner, your phone, your family calendar- wherever you write down your "to do" list.

- Be sure you keep the momentum and fun going! Add stickers when you complete the task. Draw a happy face, a thumbs-up, an exclamation point.

- Take out your journal and reflect a bit on your progress. How were you feeling before you even began this program? What were some of the emotions you were having? How was your brain fog? How long were you able to walk, run, sustain an active heart rate on your first day? Now write down how you are feeling today. Are you satisfied? Are you feeling a sense of pride and accomplishment? Do you recognize your growth no matter how small it may appear? What worked for you? Where do you need to refine your goals? Did you try something new? If so, how do you feel about that?

Continued on next page.

- Take a moment to give yourself a pat on the back. YOU did this. No one did it for you. This is the part I speak of when I suggest that you dig deep within and bring out your fighting side. Deep inside, you DO have exactly what it takes to live an optimal life!

- Remember that you are working on progress, not perfection. If you miss a day, move on. No sense in beating yourself up over it. Look at what you HAVE completed rather than what you have not. Stay focused on the positive.

	Day 1	Day 2	Day 3	Day 4	Day 5	Day 6	Day 7
8-3 School							
3-5 Practice							
5-6 Dinner							
6-7 Workout 7-10 Homework 10-10:30 Shower, quiet time							

CHAPTER FIVE
Reframing Our Greatest Learning Tools: Mistakes & Failure

Failure. The word is gross. We hear the word and think, "*ugh.*" A deep pit forms in our stomachs, feelings of regret and shame boil over, shoulders slouch. The word rears its ugly face and weasels its way into our everyday lives: Failed relationship, failed exam, failure to load. We often attach this word to our academic performances: quizzes, tests, semester grades. We feel shame. We buckle.

But we have another option. We can buck up!

Mistakes Can Be Wonderful Teachers

Thomas J. Leonard, one of the most effective personal coaches in the U.S., has this to say in *The Portable Coach*[19] about mistakes and failure: "Faults are rich and wonderful teachers. Mistakes are golden. Weaknesses are usually just hidden strengths," he says. Then he warns that those who try to live perfect lives are self-deluded and zombie-like with clenched fists. (Sounds like a creature out of a horror show.) Leonard goes on to say that we do not need to be perfect, but yes, we do need to evolve. "Get to know 100% of YOU," he says, "just as you are, with an attitude of loving-kindness."[18] And that is the attitude I want you to offer yourself each time you make a mistake or feel like you have failed at something.

Take Time to See the Big Picture

I once had a student who "failed" a quiz. He earned 3 out of 5 points. He earned 60% on this quiz. This grade threw him into a major tailspin. He couldn't see the big picture. All he could see was the "F." The result nearly devastated him; his perspective towards the class changed and his attitude towards me soured. He even wanted to change teachers!

How did this one quiz impact this student so badly? Initially, I believed his response to this grade seemed a little over the top. But I have learned that what I think doesn't matter. What truly matters is how my students process information. Some students do overreact to failing a single quiz. When you don't perform "well" on a given quiz or test, it's hard to see the big picture with any perspective—at least at first. You will not always have people in your life who will help you to break your situation down so that you can get that much-needed perspective. That's why I am teaching you how to do this for yourself.

You Can Choose Your Response!

So tell me something! Can you remember a moment when one quiz, one phone call, one text defined your day or week? Or your most important relationship? I have an example. A friend of mine says she will always remember a phone call from a hospital ER telling her that her mother passed away from a heart attack. This did define her week. Losing a loved one is vastly different from failing one quiz. But both were unexpected. The point is life will happen in big ways and in small, and some things are out of our control. While I am not one to use cliches, I can't resist the curveball here, because it is so on point. "When life throws you a curveball..." What will you do? How will you respond? Will you duck or cry? Like a curveball, some things in life will be out of our control. But we can choose our response. We can choose our reaction. We can put on a long face that we wear for the next month. Or stay in bed and cower under our blankets all weekend. No one will deny you that right. Or we can hit that curveball out of the park.

See Each Failed Moment as an Opportunity to Grow

Whether we see it or not at the time, every step on our life journey comes with a lesson. The failed quiz, the phone call with news of a loved one's passing. The curveball. Those unexpected moments. When you put your head down on your pillow at night, who do you want to be in response to that moment? Whether you realize it or not at the time, you see in the weeks or months ahead, how each event offers an opportunity to grow. So the next time disappointment happens, dig deep and say, "I am going to turn this moment around and look for the lesson. I am not a failure. I had *a failed moment.*" Remember, you already have it in you to be great. Remember what we discussed in this book's first chapter about the "acorn theory," and author James Hillman's belief that everyone comes into the world with a particular destiny, a calling, a seed of greatness that should be nourished over time by parents and teachers and mentors and self. And that no matter how many challenges you have in life, that calling—your purpose—still finds its way. Hillman says that cultures all over the world, except for America, have this same basic understanding.

When Failure Closes One Door, Stand Ready for New Possibilities

A few pages ahead, we will look at how society has warped the concept of *failure.* Before we see what the experts have to say, let's put our heads together and redefine the concept. Let's take the word apart and made sense out of it. Let's break it down: The origin of the word comes from the mid 17th century and means "the cessation of supply." Simply put, "to cease" means to stop. So think about the word "failure;" it means the stopping of an act or process. A failed act. A failed process. To fail can close a door. A hope. A dream. A plan. But guess what that does? It opens your mind to new possibilities. And we know from reading the introduction to this guide that our new mindset is in The Here and Now. This is a call to action. Restart. Refresh.

Think about your computer. If a page fails to load, what do you do? Shut your device and find something else to do? I doubt it. My guess is that you are persistent. You reload, check your wifi/internet connection, reboot, turn on a personal hotspot. The list could go on. You're so resilient and you're determined. Approach your life with the same veracity!

We Learn from Our Mistakes When We Take Time to Reflect

So please take time to reflect! What caused the malfunction? Lack of commitment? Lack of understanding? Overconfidence? Pinpoint your role in the attempt. Do not blame the teacher or the test. While I can certainly appreciate that some tests are poorly written and some teachers may include information that wasn't covered in class, it's too easy to shift the blame onto someone else, walk away and never have resolve. We are addressing your role. Look inward. After all, this is your journey.

Create an Action Plan that Yields Better Results!

Once you've determined your role, create a future plan. How will you behave differently? What will you change? Do you need a quieter work environment? Do you need more time?

Do you need a tutor? What is going to give you the best possible outcome where genuine learning takes place? Can you see how taking control over your actions (which is all you can control anyway) will improve your self confidence, skills and outcome?

Keep Your Thoughts Positive

Mahatma Gandhi, a leader in India who was known for peaceful change, offers these wise, inspiring words:

"Your beliefs become your thoughts,
Your thoughts become your words,
Your words become your actions,
Your actions become your habits,

Your habits become your values,
Your values become your destiny."

I say to you, believe in the process. Take the word, "failure," and redefine it. Make it fluid and flexible so that it works in your given mindset.

Do Your Personal Best

Another attitude worth addressing is the mindset of *not trying* or *not putting in a full- on effort.* To slack. To loaf. Have you ever done that? Maybe you do this often. I think it's largely due to fear of failure. The thought becomes, "If I don't try, then the outcome doesn't really matter. It wasn't my best, so who cares?" This is a mask and it's time to remove it.

So here's the scary part. What if you try your hardest next time. You give 100% and still fall short of your goal? What if you expected an "A" and you earned a "C?" What if you hoped for a "C" and receive an "F?"

SO WHAT!! Does those scenarios make you a failure? No. No. And NO!

We are not a letter grade. We are made up of so much more than our intellect. Settling for a C doesn't mean you are an average person. What it means is this: On that one assignment, you learned an average amount of information.

But it could mean other things, too. It could mean you had a difficult time with the test format, but can improve with practice. It could mean that you have a reading challenge that you have not yet discovered. (One of the best dentists I know had dyslexia throughout school; and a doctor who became a world respected head of a Big-Ten Ophthalmology Department did, too!) The grade could mean that you didn't study, or that you needed to study harder or differently. The point is this—no matter what it means, the letter grade only tells part of the story, reflects only one iota of your total person. In the grand scheme of life, this letter "C" will have little impact.

Your Inner Beauty Outshines Every Flaw

To illustrate, I would like you to picture a huge field of sunflowers. In your mind, visualize thousands and thousands of sunflowers. Bright yellow heads facing the sun, dancing in the wind. Standing together, they are deeply rooted and making a magical show of themselves. Did you happen to notice the one that was not as tall as the others? The one below the surface struggling for the sunlight? No, of course not. You were so taken by the beauty of that whole glorious field! The one minor flaw was insignificant.

You, my dear, are just like the field of sunflowers. You are made up of so many beautiful parts, that one minor flaw (like an unexpectedly low grade on a quiz) does not ruin the entire field of beauty. Come to see that about yourself.

Think, too, how that field came to be. Someone planted the seeds, or they were carried by the wind and took root. They had plenty of water, sun, shade and breeze to help foster them to their beautiful selves. They had challenges, but stood up to windstorms, frost and drought. Then came the worst challenge of all. Sunflower moths that nibbled away little by little, bit by bit, finally destroying them all. The flowers didn't stand a chance. But you, my friend, are different. You have a choice. Will you let in the sunflower moths to eat away at your worth? Or do you want to stand tall—*and despite the hardships*—put forth your best effort so that you can continue to grow and to flourish? Give life your personal best each day?

Begin Each Day With This Positive Affirmation. Jot these wise words[19] about failure on a sticky note and post it on your bathroom mirror! Write it on a notecard to carry in your pocket to read throughout your day!

Be Open to What Life Teaches Us Each Day

One of life's great mysteries is how we learn so much from every experience. We don't always get to pick and choose what happens in our day. But we can choose to be open and receptive to lessons from each experience in our life. Who knows beforehand what a certain assignment may inspire inside of you? Consider this! Maybe the math assignment you're learning is actually a lesson *for you* on being vulnerable, on asking for help, or for reaching out to a classmate. Asking for help shows humility and strength and that you are strong enough to admit that you don't have all of the answers, a lesson that will serve you the rest of your life. Something powerful to consider! As time passes, you'll also see that all things are connected and that all experiences will tie into the bigger picture in some way, shape, or form.

Still Frustrated?
Try This Journaling Exercise

Maybe at this point you think, *I don't know.* I tried everything and nothing is ever going to change. Ask yourself if that is really true. Then just sit with this question for 24 hours.

- If you remain at a complete loss, even after giving the situation 24 hours, I'd like you to journal a bit. "What is something about myself I am happier with now than I was one year ago?" and "What might I have done differently in a certain situation to change the outcome?"

- Put the journal away for another 24 hours.

- Once you've rested and some time has passed, reread what you have written. Is this still true?

Chances are highly likely that you do have more clarity. Remember, you picked up this guide to help yourself. Your awareness is growing, and you are making small changes step-by-step. You are doing the hard work of becoming exactly who you were meant to be! The best part is...you do not need to go far to find the answers. They live in your heart and your head.

If you want to do what you've always done, you can. No one will stop you. However, I know in my heart, you want more. You wouldn't be reading this if you didn't. So find a minor change you are willing to make, and consider that a victory! This is about progress in the right direction. *You* taking control of your destiny. This is about *you* tapping into what is right in your life and making it work for you. The promise. Your birthright.

Society's Concept of Failure Blocks Dreams and Progress

In this chapter, we've looked at the concept of failure from a few different angles. Now I would like you to look at how a narrow, negative view of failure blocks progress and our dreams. In his article on society's need to rebrand the word "failure," entrepreneur Daniel Epstein says,

"The fear of failure stops too many great minds from creating something meaningful in the world. It halts too many of us from living extraordinary lives. Fear of failure has prevented people from falling in love, becoming artists, telling friends the truth, and chasing dreams without apology. If we are going to continue to shy away from failure, it's time we redefined it."

A Mistake is Simply a Misstep on the Path to Greatness.

But our culture tells you that not only have you made a mistake or erred, but you've also committed the biggest fault of your life: EPIC FAIL. Forever. Come on, now. That notion that whatever went wrong can single-handedly define the rest of your life...it isn't honest. Let's use a car as an example. Yours or your parents or guardians. The headlight goes out. Will you fix it and love that car again, or sell it for scrap metal? I'm guessing you'll seize that moment of grace. The same holds true for humans. One defeat is not the final destination. I tell my own children all of the time that there is absolutely nothing they can *ever* do that will make me stop loving them. We deserve the gift of unconditional love.

Self Awareness is a Process

Remember what I said earlier about mistakes? A mistake is simply a misstep on the path to greatness. This is not permission to go out and to live hog wild and to be totally reckless. However, it *is* permission for you to be human, to make mistakes.

Failures provide us opportunities to experience growth. When we grow, we change our lives. We adjust our paths to greatness. We fine tune the moments that used to set us back. Those blips in our lives do not define who we are, or who we are called to be in this life. Having a newfound self awareness means you accept yourself where you are today. You appreciate that other changes will occur in the future and you accept that you may have made decisions in the past that do not fully reflect the person you want to become. This is true of any human, because self awareness is a process.

It's important to remember, too, that being self-aware does not mean being selfish. You still have a responsibility to be kind to others. You still have a responsibility to follow through on commitments. You still have a responsibility to honor all humans.

What Would You Like to Change the Most?

One of the most beautiful parts of our humanity is accepting ourselves where we are- flaws and all. After all, we all make mistakes sometimes and we all need a little redirection. So take time to look at the parts of your life you would like to change the most. What can you do about it? Write it on a notecard, put it in your pocket and look at it several times each day.

    A few examples:

- I will wake up each day and remind myself to be grateful for three things in life.

- Each time I begin to worry or think negative thoughts, I will replace that thinking with a positive thought, such as, "I know all will be well." (This doesn't mean each day will be perfect; it means you will manage to get through whatever challenges you face.)

- Instead of complaining, I will do two kind things for others today.

- I will commit to reviewing one-hour a week what I've learned in each class that week.

- I will walk with confidence, knowing the people who love me have my back.

A Simple Change in Attitude Can Change Your Life

I tell my kids all the time that *what we think about we bring about.* If we manifest greatness, we will be great. The next time you are up against a challenge, visualize the outcome. See yourself being successful, radiant and happy. Know that you have the power within you to be great. It is your birthright. Did you know that? I certainly did not realize when I was a teenager that God, the divine, your Higher Power, the universe- whatever you want to call the spiritual guiding force in your life- wants you to be happy, prosperous and full of joy. Each of us is on a specific path. We have to want the best for ourselves.

> **If you have a hard time doing this, try this visual.**
> *Picture a small child swinging on the swings. She falls off and has tears rolling down her cheeks. You're within arms' length of her. What do you do? You reach for her, don't you? You do so because that is a natural reaction to a child in pain. You respond to people in a way that shows kindness, care and concern.*

This is true of us in the universe. When we are in pain or feel sad or misguided, some force outside of us is cheering for us. Some force wants to reach for us and to wipe our tears away. You are no different than the little child on the swing. So be assured that a power beyond you wants what is best. You don't have to feel it, or see it, or know it. All you have to do is have faith that it is out there reaching for you. Take comfort in knowing that no matter what "failure" you've experienced, you will be okay. You are never ever alone.

PLUGGING IN PRACTICE:

- Stop: Get in a quiet place and set a timer for five minutes and put your phone away.
  (Out of sight, out of mind.)

- Take in a big deep breath and exhale slowly to calm your mind. Do so five times.

- Identify the feeling or emotion you have. If it's negative, give yourself permission to let that feeling go. Staying negative is not going to serve you, nor keep you on your path to greatness.

- Visualize change: How do you see yourself being successful? Picture yourself tweaking your action plan and getting the result you want.

- Believe in yourself.

- Think of one experience you used to view as a failure that you can now see as one of life's greatest lessons. What did you learn?

- Remind yourself that your past mistakes do not dictate your future successes.

FINAL PLUGS:

1. Ask for help. We are not created to be alone and to know it all.

2. Be gentle on yourself. Sometimes this path is like a maze with all kinds of turns and corners. No one gets it "right" the first time.

3. Remind yourself that peace, joy, contentment and happiness are your birthright. While no one is meant to be happy all the time, we can be happy at least once a day, and we can grow our attitudes of joy, peace, and contentment.

4. Know that you are seen. You are the sum of ALL your parts, and you are beautiful for each of them.

5. Be in your own race. Life is not about what you have; it's about who you are.

6. Tap into the divine within you. Settle yourself and listen to your higher good.

CHAPTER SIX
The Food → Mood Connection: Take Charge of Your Cravings!

Many of you have probably heard the expression, "You are what you eat." Never is this more true than in today's world, especially in the U.S. where one-third of the adult population is obese. The U.S. is known for poor eating habits, but teens are increasingly taking charge of their health and nutrition. How well do you think you eat? If you were to keep a food journal over the course of the next week, would you be surprised to learn that what you are putting *in your mouth* may not be the best plan for your body? Or do you think you make healthy choices?

Certain Foods Trigger Brain Fog

Studies have shown that there is a direct correlation between mood and food. Brain fog is something many teens can relate to. Many times this is a direct result of what we are consuming. If we took a step back and changed even one meal a day for a week, the results would be astounding: clearer skin, improved sleep, better liver function to help clean toxins, stronger nails, stronger hair. Our brain needs good, healthy, high-density proteins for optimal function.

Less Brain Fog Means Greater Mental Clarity

When we eat processed, sugar-filled foods and drink sugar-infused, caffeinated coffees, we deprive our bodies of our best effort. Whole foods, food that are organic, non-gmo, and not filled with hidden sugars provide better choices for our body. So what does this mean? Do you have to convince your mom or dad or whoever buys the groceries in your house to go all-organic? Do you have to swear off fries forever? NO! All things in moderation. You start small. You can do this by beginning to increase your water intake. Something as simple as increasing your hydration can have a huge impact on your brain function. Your cells need to be fed and you do this by drinking water. "Well," you say, "I hate water!"

Small Changes, Big Pay-Off!
Let's take a moment here to ask a few critical questions: Why are you reading this book? Isn't it to better yourself? You wouldn't have made it this far into the pages unless you had some desire within you to enact change. I don't mean drastic changes all at once. Even small change brings big results. You have the glorious gift of free will. So, you can continue to drink and eat what you want. Or you can commit to change. I don't mean drastic changes all at once. Even small change brings big results. But the change must be specific. It's not enough to say, "I'm going to eat better." Instead, commit to small, specific changes that you can track. If you really do want to live your best life now, take minor steps and make small (bite-sized, ha!) concessions to get there. Here are three examples of manageable nutrition goals:

- *I will drink at least eight glasses (or three water bottles) of water every day.*

- *I will cut out (or cut back on) beverages that have sugar and artificial sweeteners.*

- *I will have only one cup of coffee each morning.*

You can actually track these changes, and you should feel positive benefits in less than a week!

Do you think anyone who has achieved good eating habits did so simply by wishing for change? Heck no! Do you think they were all Olympic contenders? No way! They made little changes in the *here and now* that paid huge dividends later in life. You, too, can commit to small change for big results!

So drink more water. Plain, good-old fashioned water. Try to fill it up a water bottle at least three times a day. More than that and you're crushing it!

Meet Fruit and Veggie Challenge Head On

The FDA recommends five to seven servings of fruit and vegetables a day. Most people eat far less. I could recommend sneaking these foods into your food plan, but I know you are stronger than that. I know you can take this challenge *to eat better* head on. Find the fruits you do like and eat plenty of them. The same goes for vegetables.

If you have a palate that dislikes the textures, then trick yourself and use a juicer, a food processor, a blender, anything you can to break those fruits and vegetables down so you can drink them instead. Remember, whatever it takes. If for some reason, you cannot add enough fruit and veggies into your meal plan, ask your doctor about taking a multivitamin.

Eat Protein to Curb Food Cravings

Finally, remember to get the protein your growing body needs. Protein comes in many forms and you can find excellent articles on healthy protein choices. If you are vegetarian or vegan, you will find many complete protein sources. Even if you love meat, for better health and variety, try to also work in vegetarian sources of protein. Did you know that having protein at breakfast helps to curb food cravings throughout the day. Protein also increases muscle mass, a process which can rev up your metabolism. If you plan to buy protein powder to help to increase the levels of protein you're getting each day, thoroughly research this, as some brands come with harmful ingredients.

Many articles on food cravings have found that our cravings

often tell us that our body needs something nutritionally that we are not getting in our diet. The next time you find yourself craving chocolate or carrots or bread, learn what these cravings mean. Natasha Longo has written about the various messages embedded in our food cravings.[20]

As you embark on this nutritional journey, remind yourself that you are eating better because you ARE better! You are worth every step of this journey. Just like you need meditation and prayer for your soul, you need to feed your body properly too. Think of the mantra, *"Good in, Good out."* (Yes, I know what you are thinking, but here is my point!) If you put good food in, you are going to produce good results.

You Have the Power to Ripple Goodness

This is also true for thoughts. If you think good thoughts, you will speak good thoughts. If you speak good thoughts, you will act accordingly. It's a cycle that becomes contagious! By complimenting the cashier on good service, smiling at a stranger, holding the door for someone, even when it's out of your comfort zone or may slow you down a whole four seconds, think of the ripple effect: You feel good about your actions. You've made someone else feel good, too. And guess what? They will pay it forward, and so on, and so on. And all because you smiled.

Commit to Healthy Breakfast

Be sure to eat breakfast. I don't care if it's a banana. Put something healthy in your body to get your brain going. Something besides sugary cereals and Poptarts! Some nutritional experts will also tell you to start with some hot water and a bit of lemon. This helps to get things moving along the intestinal tract if you catch my drift. It's natural and is a good solution to waking your body up naturally. Ideally, a whole grain cereal that is high in protein with some organic milk and a serving of organic fruit on top is an excellent start. If you have to have bacon, some turkey bacon with your free-range eggs will do. Have some high calcium orange juice (watch the sugar on the label) and off you go.

Benefits of A Brown-Bag Lunch

Okay, back to eating healthy and the benefit of packing your own lunch, especially if your school doesn't offer healthy choices. You don't have to use brown bags either. My kids each have lunchboxes. One of my friends said she used to bring her lunch in a Wonder Woman lunch box. Do what works for you and pack it the night before so you aren't rushed in the morning. If you have siblings, have them make a lunch with you. It's always more fun when you have someone to share time with when you're first starting a new habit. If your parent works outside of the home, encourage them to make a lunch too. You might even get an assembly line going so one person washes the fruit, slices it and bags it while another is making sandwiches or pouring single servings of salad dressing into reusable containers. If you are in an after school sport or club, add a snack to eat after your last class and before your event.

The best things about packing my lunch is that I can control ingredients and portions! I typically have a salad that is high in protein (eggs), lots of lettuce and some veggies. The dressing I choose is low in sugar and high in natural fats. Olive oil and balsamic vinegar mixed together is pretty darn tasty. I always throw in two pieces of fruit and a small serving of nuts (dry almonds, cashews, sunflower seeds, etc.). I also throw in an organic decaf or herbal tea bag as an afternoon treat. Add in a refillable water bottle and I am good to go. This kind of lunch is filled with energy, antioxidants, and powerful food for my brain. I work with teenagers (Yes, YOU!), so I need all the energy I can get and I have to stay sharp! By not filling up on sugar and caffeine I don't crash at 3:00 p.m. In fact, I am ready to take on the after-school meeting, the kids' activities, my commute and whatever work I need to complete that evening- all because I ate well. In this way, I also honor and respect my body. We all deserve love and respect from ourselves; honoring our bodies with healthy food habits is one way to show self-respect.

Want More Money and Better Health? Dump Big Name Coffee Houses!

I'm going to take a side bar and speak to those of you who "have" to have your Big Name Coffee. It doesn't make you cool. These companies may not like what I have to say, but I have witnessed the impact for years, have done my research and now I am exercising my right to free speech. You're spending anywhere from $4 to $9 on a sugary drink that doesn't do a darn thing for your body, except to spike your insulin and cause a sugar and caffeine high. By your third period class, you are dragging and cannot recall what you've already learned. You hear yourself saying, "Ugh. I am SO tired. I barely slept last night. I NEED a nap." What? You're a teenager! Listen to what you are telling yourself day in and day out! What's more, I speak from experience. For years, I put sugar and caffeine in my body at a huge price financially and physically. It fogged my brain, wore me out and drained me. I felt like I needed a nap by late morning every day! I'm guessing the same is true for you!

This doesn't make good sense now does it?

But like Albert Einstein said, the definition of insanity is doing the same thing over and over and expecting different results. Buying overpriced, sugar-spiked coffee with artificial ingredients, and expecting to feel wholly energized all day is an unrealistic expectation. Hello, sugar crash!

The National Institute on Drug Abuse for Teens (Yes, caffeine is a stimulant drug!) relays great evidence on the impact of caffeine in this article: "The Buzz on Caffeine," by Sara Bellum.[21]

If that doesn't convince you, add up how many times you go to one of those high-priced coffee joints on average in a week. Now multiply that by 52 weeks in a year, and multiply that by the average cost of your coffee. Venti caramel macchiato will set you back $5.49 (depending on the region.) In a year, you've spent $856.44, and that's only three times a week and doesn't include any muffins or extras you may be enticed into buying. Over your high school career that's $3,424.00! A decent down payment on a new or used car, or a special trip after graduation. Overpriced coffee should be a treat; not a necessity. Practice some self-restraint and you'll be happier in the end. I get that it's a social thing. You can still go with your friends and be social. Tell yourself you aren't missing out, and you aren't depriving yourself. Rather you're saving up for an enormously special gift for yourself, instead of those short bursts of gratification. Change the behavior and you will change the outcome. Learning how to delay your gratification will serve you well in this life.

Small Steps → Colossal Benefits

Aside from eating properly, you can fuel your desires and achieve your goals in many other ways, including positive thinking. Some people have labeled this the Law of Attraction, which is the focus of *The Secret*,[22] a book by author Rhonda Byrne. This theory basically says, "What we think about, we bring about." More on this in Chapter 8, but for now, as you focus on healthy eating, remember the power of our thoughts. Ask yourself, what do you want? Who do you want to be? What are your interests? When do you feel good about yourself? What triggers you to respond with joy, happiness, and passion? Tapping into these feelings will really lay the groundwork for something great in your life. I often tell my students when they approach life from a place of love, they cannot go wrong. So get yourself in a quiet spot and really think about what fuels you.

PLUGGING IN PRACTICE:

1. **Keep a food journal for three days.** Use the Food Chart I've included at the end of this chapter on page 65. Write directly on it, or if you'd like to use it again in the future, duplicate it in your journal. After three days, take a look at your chart.

   • What patterns have you found?

   • Do you start the day off great and then turn to sugar at lunch or after school?

   • Are you getting enough fruits and vegetables?

   • How is your water intake?

   • Most importantly, where can you make adjustments?

   • We are not looking to overhaul every area of your life in a week. Plan to make minor tweaks here and there until they become habit. Commit to one area that you are willing to improve in your diet, set a goal, and for the next 21 days, commit to that goal, that new bit of good health for yourself.

2. **Write your new health goal down on the Health Goal chart.** Over the next three weeks, put a check after each day that you are successful. If you miss a day, no big deal. Pick back up and look at each day as a new beginning. As you start your plan, keep three things in mind:

• Be realistic. Losing 10 pounds in three weeks is not realistic nor healthy. You cannot sustain that kind of weight loss.

Continued on the next page.

- All things in moderation. We set ourselves up for failure if we say we are swearing off sugar 100%. So set yourself up for success. Be willing to learn about sugar's harmful effect, and be willing to cut back.

- Be kind to yourself. If you find yourself engaging in self-deprecating thoughts, STOP. Get your sticky notes to remind yourself you have worth, you are valuable and you are on a path to greatness.

3. Water Challenge: I said all things in moderation. Water is the exception! Commit to drinking water all day in place of the other liquids you typically drink. No soda, no sports drinks, no coffee, no energy drinks. Pure water. How many ounces did you consume? Now compare that number to yesterday? Is it higher? Then, you are on the right track! If it's lower, be vigilant as to how you feel. If you had a soda, did it make you feel sluggish? Don't beat yourself up over it. Look at the times you treated your body kindly. Again, this is not a contest. This is YOU making small changes that will have a big impact on your health and your mood!

	Breakfast	Lunch	Dinner	Snack
Day One				
Day Two				
Day Three				

4. My Health Goal is: _____

_____

_____

I will achieve this goal by _____

_____

1._____	12._____
2._____	13._____
3._____	14._____
4._____	15._____
5._____	16._____
6._____	17._____
7._____	18._____
8._____	19._____
9._____	20._____
10_____	21._____
11._____	

CHAPTER SEVEN
Social Media Aside, Learn to "Like" Your Irresistible Self!

Facebook, Twitter, Snapchat, Instagram & Pinterest. Hacks. Scams. The most private of matters going viral. Job loss. Cyberbullying. Sadly, even loss of life. Lack of privacy controls. Maybe you knew it before Facebook CEO Mark Zuckerberg went on his most recent apology tour. Social media has its good and bad sides. Unfortunately, many youths get sucked into social media at such a young age (sometimes as young as kindergarten) that their good judgment has not yet developed. And once social media use becomes habit, it's hard to stop craving.

But you are not entirely at fault; you are a product of our tech culture. Consequently, regardless of your gender you have easy access and more exposure to pornography, sex, violence, an unrealistic norm for popularity, "beauty," and the "ideal" body. (How many filters are used on the pictures you've seen? You'll never know!) Your life is one big social media interruption. You might even feel as though you lack face-to-face communication skills. And you judge yourself by how many "likes" you get.

Mindless Scrolling: The Digital Rabbit Hole
Don't get me wrong, it's pretty great to share fun events like a concert, or a great book you've just read. But get real. How many teens do you know who limit their use of social media?

You mindlessly scroll through the posts, then stop, and think, "Wow. Must be nice to have a family take you on a beach vacation.

My family never does that." Wait. A. Minute. What's wrong with your family? Your friend's post doesn't show the truth of that vacation. People post the good and not what's wrong in their lives. Maybe their parents charged the vacation and are running up huge credit card debts. Maybe their parents allowed them to drink on that vacation and your friend got really sick. Or worse. Maybe the family fought half the time. No one posts the truth. Think of the times times you posted. Was it when you were in full makeup with your hair perfect? Did you edit the photo for just the right lighting? Did you take 18 pics to get it right? Were you Googling "cute captions for vacay photos" so you sound clever?

A Call to Teen Activism! Stand Up to Sexism and Stereotypes!
Aside from the damage social media does to a person's self esteem, social media and many apps continue to perpetuate sexism and stereotyping. Yet, every time you log onto Google, you fall prey to both. For example, multi-player games generally include free characters; the majority are male. Siri, Alexa, and the other 'helper" apps default to female voices. Why is this? Can't men be helpful? Teens hate being stereotyped! It's time that your generation takes a look at the "truths" the technology industry is selling to you subliminally. Tech companies spend millions of dollars a year on test markets and know how to target age groups. Take back your role in this and refuse to play along. Stand up for what's right and believe that your generation can and will make a huge impact on how tech operates. Do a little digging and see for yourself how you are being a target. Make a decision that you will not be a victim of advertising targets and that you are a knowledgeable consumer who does her research.

I want you to understand WHY we have this non-stop urge to post, "like," share and scroll! The answer? The one I touched on in Chapter Three: that *dopamine rush.*[23] That same neurochemical released after certain actions or behaviors, like winning a race or doing well on an exam. Read the following excerpt to see how advertisers use this information to THEIR financial advantage! Yes, advertisers want YOU...and your money! And they want you to click on "like" to their advantage!

According to a study of Australian consumers by San Francisco-based media-buying firm RadiumOne, social media usage is a dopamine gold mine. "Every time we post, share, 'like,' comment or send an invitation online, we are creating an expectation," according to the study. "We feel a sense of belonging and advance our concept of self through sharing."[23]

These findings are significant! They help explain why we feel compelled to frequently click "like." Equally important, the findings reveal the power that marketers hold by creating social content we can like and share.

Social Media "Likes" Create Isolation

Think about it! How many times have you posted and checked back several times an hour to see how many *likes* you've gotten? This is damaging to your soul. The more likes you get, the more valuable you feel. The less likes you get, the less valuable you feel. Self doubt creeps in. *Maybe it didn't post right. Maybe people just aren't online right now. Surely my friends would like this.* Or even worse, *Well she's such a B**, she never likes my pics anyway because she's jealous.* And while part of that may be true, getting yourself wrapped up in what other people think of our posts is hurting you. You cannot judge yourself by *how you think* "others" want you to be. Your life and your self worth are an inside job. Looking externally causes hurt, shame, and low self esteem.

Also, this isn't reality. Social media creates a fake environment that is no different than the false promise of the beer commercials: *Everyone looks great, they are all happy and content, and life is perfect.* If this is true, Friend, then why would researchers find a connection between the use of social media and a rise in teen suicide? One student in Colorado was so concerned with teen suicides in her town, that she created a campaign called *Offline October*. Her campaign spread worldwide and had amazing results. I had my high school students participate and keep informal notes in their journals. The results amazed them, too. "I felt better about myself." "I spent more time outdoors." (or with my parents or with my siblings) "I slept better." "Felt I focused on my homework and understood it better."

Stay True to What is Real

Remember that the divine made one very specific and special path just for you. When we get caught up in comparisons, it is like telling the universe, "I don't like your plan for me. I want something better." Stop putting your energy into negative thinking and focus on finding who you are meant to be. Stay true to what feels pure and genuine. I promise if you do your personal best, Good will follow. Our goal in this lifetime is to be happy. Happiness is your own inner feeling of joy. Happiness is NOT, as the media and advertising have brainwashed you into thinking, the new phone, the better car, the best skin, the perfect body. That simply isn't true. We don't *have* to have any of those things. We need to refocus our attention on what brings us joy and peace.

PLUGGING IN PRACTICE:
Read and Write: Reflecting on Your Purpose

Recall in Chapter 1 when I invited you to identify your gift and special meaning in life? Now is a good time to review and to see meaning from a different perspective. Here is a link to a recent article by Shannon Kaiser on finding your life purpose: *3 Unexpected Ways to Find Your Life Purpose* **https://www.huffingtonpost.com/shannon-kaiser/3-unexpected-ways-to-find_b_5176511.html)**[24]

- What new thoughts or insights do you have about your purpose in life after reading Kaiser's article? Write about this in your journal.

As you are seeking your true purpose, one of your greatest gifts is learning to love life and to love who you are TODAY. We're not looking ahead to when you lose the weight, get more buff, grow your hair. None of that. We love ourselves today. Yes, we will work hard to take care of (and to honor and respect) our bodies, but we will also work on seeing the positive in ourselves—*and in others*—each and every day. The more we do this, the less mental space we have to worry about what others think! Keep in mind that Jesus (who some see as Savior and others see as a prophet) had only 12 official followers. Who said you need 1,000?

The world's opinion does not matter. Not today.

PLUGGING IN PRACTICE:
Write responses to the following in your journal

- For one day, keep track of how many times you are on social media.

- Process: How did you feel when you were scrolling? Did you feel judgmental, jealous, envious, snarky? Why do you think you felt that way?

- Proceed: Make a commitment to cut your time online down by one-half. This includes any social media. Yes, even Pinterest! Do you have FOMO? Sounds like an illness, right? And in a way it is. FOMO is anxiety (Fear of Missing Out) some teens and young adults experience when they see social media posts showing exciting or interesting events happening elsewhere.

- This is a good time to be honest; you're working on you. Now that you've cut back on social media, how do you feel? Many people feel a little lonely for a period of time until they engage in other activities. Do you feel anxious? Bored?

- Maybe you're wandering around and just not sure what to do with your time. Decide what you'd love to do instead with your free time. Wander with purpose! In other words, go for a walk! How did you feel after your walk?

- Hone your skills on new hobbies and activities you've always wanted to try! Do you want to workout? Try calligraphy or painting? Tae Kwon Do or table tennis? Chess or cooking? Maybe you think it would be cool to create some chalkboard art or signs. Do you have an older relative you'd like to visit...face-to-face? Now is the time to do so. (You will make their day!) If any of these ideas appeal to you, what action steps (did) will you take to get started?

- Your list of options is endless! Looking back, you will be amazed at how much time you used to spend online. In time, you are going to learn how fabulous it is to live in the real world, in the here-and-now. One of my students told me how freeing it was for her to put her phone down and go outside for a run. "I just felt so free, unattached and open to listening to myself and my thoughts," she said. She was uncomfortable at first- and that's okay. Change IS uncomfortable. But the outcome is amazing.

- For the next three weeks, revisit the questions at the end of Chapter 7. Write responses in your journal, and compare your responses from week to week. Has anything changed in your life? If so, write about it!

CHAPTER EIGHT
Self Love Sets Foundation for Positive Changes in Your Life

I open this chapter with an empowering yet gentle directive from Lois McMaster Bujold, science fiction writer and mother of two: "Don't wish to be normal. Wish to be yourself. To the hilt. Find out what you're best at, and develop it, and hopscotch your weaknesses. Wish to be great at whatever you are."[25] Don't you love what she is saying? Bypass your weaknesses as you focus on your strengths!

You'll want to keep your journal handy all through this chapter. Unlike most of the other chapters, where practice comes at the end, the Plugging In Practice is embedded throughout this chapter.

PLUGGING IN PRACTICE:

- Now read Bujold's quotation again. Depending on where you are, read silently or aloud. Read slower than usual. Take time as you read to hear or imagine your voice as you emphasize each word. Let each word sink into your heart.

- In your journal, write what you think and feel when you read Bujold's quotation.

Multifaceted Beautiful You
To be yourself, as Bujold suggests, you should know who you are. It is not uncommon for teens and young adults to have questions about their identity. Who you are comes in many forms and is comprised of many definitions. These include:

1. Family of origin

2. Genetics and heredity

3. Your religious affiliation (until you're old enough to decide)

4. Your neighborhood

5. Your sexual preference, gender identity

6. Your inner (or intrinsic) values and beliefs

7. Your job (assuming you have one)

8. Your extrinsic likes and dislikes (external or outside forces)

9. Your friends

10. Your reputation

11. Your interests and hobbies

12. Your club, sports, teams, affiliations

How many things on this list do you have the power to change right now, today? If you said, "Not all of them," you are right. Basically, you have the ability to change many of the areas listed, if you really want to make a change. That's pretty exciting! You do not have control over 1-5. I know I will get some backlash on this, but quite frankly, this book isn't about discussing how sexuality comes into play or one's gender identity. There are experts for that. I am not one of them. Therefore, for the sake of simplicity and inclusion, I am going to say that individuals can best recognize their own gender identity and sexual preference.

What Would You Most Like to Change to Improve Your Life?

Clearly, you cannot change everything all at once, but to begin, focus on a few areas. Think about three areas where positive change will greatly benefit you. Or ask yourself this: In what areas of your life do you feel stuck? This is a chance for a do-over!

PLUGGING IN PRACTICE:
Journal Your Path to Beneficial Change

- If I could change three things today to set myself on a stellar path, what three areas would impact my life for the best? List these three areas.

- How would each change make my life better?

- Now consider and commit to each area, one at a time. How can you best approach each change? Does it work better for you to take small, incremental steps, or will you jump in head first? What works best for you?

- No matter how you start, stay the course. Face fear head on. Do not waiver.

You Can't Change People, But You Can Change Who You Hang Out With

As you consider making positive change, let's take a minute to talk about what it means to have control over people. Do you find yourself telling others that if they only knew your boyfriend or girlfriend the way you do, they wouldn't dislike him/her? Do you tell your family and friends that the person in question never treats you poorly when you are alone?

My point is that if you are constantly making excuses for the person in your life who behaves poorly and treats you poorly, makes you feel less than you are, you need to look deep inside for the courage to leave this relationship. Whether this is a friend, boyfriend or girlfriend, you will NEVER, I repeat, NEVER change the other person. It doesn't matter if you lose weight, have more sex (gasp), shower them with gifts or money, spend more time with him/her, you will not change that person.

Be honest with yourself. No room here for self-deception. Are you putting more time and energy into worrying about the relationship than it is worth? What energy do you feel when you are with them? Positive? Negative? Do you believe you are your best self with this person? Are you?   Chances are if you are making excuses for this person's behavior, the true answer is "NO."

Call on a Trusted Adult to Help You to Leave a Harmful Relationship

American writer and activist Maya Angelou said, "If you don't like something, change it. If you can't change it, change your attitude."[26] You cannot change abusive relationships, but you can and should save yourself, and you will need a trusted adult to help you with this, so that your parting comes in a way that is safe, dignified and permanent. Once you take this step, you will have emotional space to make a few other changes in your life.

Remember Self Love!

Before you jump into changing everything around you, it is so vital to determine who you are and to develop a loving relationship with yourself. I am not advising you to be egotistical or self-absorbed. But you must: Like yourself. Respect yourself. Think of yourself in positive ways.

The gentle, yet powerful directive below says it best:
Fall In Love
With Taking
Care Of Yourself.
Mind—Body—Spirit.

For if we truly love who we are today, we can stay above the negative influences around us. We can rise above those who want to pull us down.

What Other Changes Can You Make?

Now that you have changed the most essential areas in your life, you can consider other adjustments. For example, how do you take time for yourself and your growth while still being a responsible, productive person? First and foremost, you recognize your desire to change. You get into the practice of making lists of what to do and how to go about doing them. You take an inventory of what you are currently doing and look for ways to either scale back or ways to increase the productivity in your life.

PLUGGING IN PRACTICE:
Journal to Further Explore Beneficial Changes in Your Life

- What three changes would I most like to achieve?
- As I make changes in my life, what part(s) of the process is (are) working well for me?
- What isn't serving me well?
- What can I do to serve others?

Move Forward at a Pace That Works for You

You may have just discovered some great strategies that improve your life each day, and keep you on your path to greatness. This is terrific. As you continue to grow, be gentle with yourself and realize some change will come quickly and other change will take time. The important piece to remember is that you are moving forward. I know that it seems like a lot. Trust me. In time, and with practice, self-reflection will become second nature to you.

Remember to focus on the end goal: Stepping onto your path to greatness and fulfilling your life's purpose. The old saying, "Rome wasn't built in a day" holds true for you. Brick by brick, layer by layer, you will develop and grow into a magnificent towering structure. This is what the Universe intended for you.

Self Love Makes for More Courageous Living

As you determine who you are and love yourself for who you are, you will find the courage and stamina to be exactly where you want to be in this life. For if we truly love who we are today, we can stay above the negative influences around us. We can rise above those who want to pull us down. We are better equipped to distinguish what is good or bad for us. Our self love radar is up and it will help to guide us along the path of goodness and toward our goals. And remember, you will succeed on your path to goodness, because the Universe really does have your back.

Wish Only to be the Best Version of Yourself

We began with Bujold's inspirational quote of the day. Her words carry power and wisdom, so let's come full circle and reiterate her wisdom: "Don't wish to be normal. Wish to be yourself. To the hilt. Find out what you're best at, and develop it, and hopscotch your weaknesses. Wish to be great at whatever you are."

CHAPTER NINE
How Best to Deal With Negative—*Toxic*—People and Comments

"The trick is to act, as far as possible, like a person who is fully secure. That is, act like someone who is respected and loved by others, and in control of the important aspects of their life."

Raj Raghunathan, Ph.D., Professor of Marketing

We are social creatures and we do react to what others have to say. It can be difficult and even hurtful to be the target of someone who is moody or pessimistic, negative or critical. While Chapter Eight touched on abusive relationships; this chapter focuses on negative comments and negative others. This chapter explores strategies to help you deal with and rise above rude, cutting comments. Negative others are often called "toxic," for their attempts to wreak havoc. In a fascinating *Psychology Today* article[27] about how to deal with negative people, the author (Raj Raghunathan, Ph.D.) digs deep into human nature and gets to the bones of this issue. He talks about why people are negative and why some solutions for dealing with them do not work. He then offers this solution:

We must remain positive and strong regardless of what others say.
When others are negative, we must
Act Secure, Respected, in Control and Loved by Others.

This is brilliant advice! I know that it's not easy to be in control when others come at us with snarky or cutting comments. Their goal is to push our buttons, and our tendency is to verbally lash back, or to feel defeated. Their exact agenda! They WANT to hijack our power and to watch us fall victim to their words. But these toxic others have no right to our time, energy or feelings. With practice, we can coach ourselves into a strong and positive state of mind!

So, the author's advice strikes me as an excellent solution. He says: "This brings me to the most tenable option for dealing with negative people. If you cannot ignore them or walk away (family members & others) the best option for dealing with negative people involves three elements: compassion (if only in your mind) for the negative person, taking responsibility for your own happiness despite the other person's negativity, and maturity in how you interact with the negative person. The trick is to act, as far as possible, like a person who is fully secure. That is, act like someone who is respected and loved by others, and in control of the important aspects of their life." Remember, we can achieve this state of mind with practice!

What Others Think of Us...Is None of Our Business!

So what if this negative person happens to be part of your social circle? I get that sometimes we get caught up in everybody else's opinion of us. The truth of the matter is that we are not responsible for other people's thoughts or opinions. Has it ever occurred to you that what other people think of us...is none of our business? I know this sounds funny, but it's true. Your own opinion of yourself is the only one that should matter to you! If you have ever been to a poster store, you'll find so many posters with beautiful backdrops, misty mountains, ocean waves, glorious sunsets, each with variations on this same message! Deepak Chopra (author, public speaker and health advocate) takes it one step further. He says: "What other people think of you is none of your business. If you start to make that your business, you will be offended the rest of your life."[28]

Remember First Lady Michele Obama's convention speech, "When they go low, we go high." So no matter what anyone says, take the high road. Decide what's best. Should you walk away? Should you ignore the comment? If not, respond in a calm manner.

Let's look at some examples of how this can go. Let's say someone negative (a family member, teacher or "friend") says to you, "You shouldn't waste your time going after that dream of yours. You'll never get there," you can simply say, "I feel differently. I feel confident. Anyway, I'd rather take a chance and fail, than not try at all." Or let's say someone negative tries to crush what you see as taking a healthy risk. She says, "You know, everyone I know who tried that ended up worse off." You can calmly respond, "We will see what happens." In fact, you can offer your most genuine smile as you say this.

How We Often Feel When We Encounter Difficult Peer Situations

You're at a football game and you see someone you used to be good friends with. She looks you up and down and whispers something to her friend and they laugh. In that moment, how do you feel? Angry? Ashamed? Vindictive? Let's play this out. So let's say you do feel vindictive. In your mind, you're calling her all kinds of bad things. You're with a new friend and you engage in mirrored behavior. You toss your hair back, add a smirk to you face and strut past. When you find your seat, you're still reeling, so you proceed to talk about her. In fact, you decide since you're not friends anymore that now would be a good time to spill some of the dirt you have on her. Knowing this will damage her reputation and because you feel hurt by her behavior, you start talking. Maybe it was a family problem she disclosed to you in private. Maybe it was a time she went too far with a guy and felt regret. It doesn't really matter what the circumstances are. The point is you start talking. You might feel instant gratification in that moment, but chances are, later when you have quiet time, you feel remorse. During that time you tell yourself that she asked for it. You aren't friends anymore so it doesn't matter. If only she'd been nice, you wouldn't have acted that way.

Hold On To Your Power!

The good news is you don't have to feel any of those things. Take the power back! Remember that you are in charge of yourself. What you do, how you act and how you think. You don't get to control how an old friend treats you. But you do get to decide how you want to behave. So go back to the football game. You see the same behavior in your friend; however, because you've practiced being in charge of your feelings and comments, you turn the situation around. You tell yourself, "I am enough. I do not need to engage in this battle." Instead of worrying, remember all of the places you are going in your life! You are on a path to greatness. You cannot allow something petty to upset you. Gossip is petty. After you've given yourself a pep talk to put yourself on the right path again, I want you to play out the whole situation in your mind. (You'll practice this not in the moment, so that when the moment *happens*, you're prepared.). This is not about being vindictive. This about staying true to you. You want to be happy, free from guilt and free from regret. No one likes to lie their head down at night and feel that knot in the pit of your stomach because they behaved poorly. You tell yourself that you are NOT going to engage in this battle. So you walk on by, smile if you can and go to your seat. From that point on, you get in the moment and you enjoy the game. And always be on guard for that inner gremlin, you know, the one who lives inside each of us. The one that tempts you to Say this! Say that! Be mean! Be vindictive! He made you feel terrible! Get even! No one made you feel anything. You are the boss of your feelings. When a situation unleashes your inner gremlin, push back! Nothing good comes from retaliation. Watch the game and be true to yourself. No revenge. No gossip. No disclosing secrets told in confidence. "Why not?" you ask. "We aren't friends anymore." That may be true, but wouldn't you rather know that even in the worst of situations you are a person of integrity? Someone whom others can trust?

Remain the Master of Your Happiness

As you practice feeling stronger and more confident, you will BECOME stronger and more confident. You will find it easier to discount negative behaviors and comments. A friend of mine had a family member going through a very difficult time. As sad as that was, he lashed out at others to help relieve some of his own stress. His counselor gave this advice to family members: "Don't let a sinking ship take you down." Isn't that great advice? My friend remembered that advice, and it served her well. Hang on to your emotional energy, your optimism, your plans for your future...so that YOU have it when you need it! No matter what toxic people say or do to hurt you, always remember that your self-worth comes from within.

PLUGGING IN PRACTICE:
Hold on to Your Power!

- Daily Affirmation: Write this on a notecard, and for the next week or two, carry it in your pocket to take out and read at least three times each day. "I am fully secure. I am respected and loved by others, and in control of the important aspects of my life." (Remember to empty your pocket at night or before doing laundry!)

- For the next week, each night before bed, read Deepak Chopra's affirmation we quoted earlier: "What Other People Think of You is None of Your Business." Say each word intentionally. Let the meaning sink in. Let these words be the last words you hear before falling asleep.

- Remind yourself that people who hurt others usually feel inferior and hurt deeply themselves. You can feel compassion and forgive, but do not accept their behavior. Maintain self-respect!

- Practice handling negative comments. Nasty comments often catch us off guard. Close your eyes and imagine yourself responding in one of the following ways:
  –Offer a genuine smile, then walk away.
  –Respond in a way that shows you have retained your power: If they try to cut you down a notch or dismiss one of your goals or ideas, you can say, "I'm certain I have what it takes, and I'm going to learn so much by trying." OR "I'm confident that this will work out for the best." OR "I'm sorry you seem out of sorts. Let's have this conversation another time." Then walk away!

Continued on next page.

- Create a Support System. Some situations require adult help. Have one or two adults you can talk to when you need a new point of view. Sometimes it helps to process or simply talk it out.

- At the end of this week, write responses to these questions in your journal: What was your biggest challenge? To what extent did your daily affirmations or other practice help you to deal with this challenge? How do you feel about the outcome?

Blogger Kute Blackson has written further about Chopra's affirmation as follows:[29]

"What Other People Think of You is None of Your Business, it's their business.

- Wasting your time thinking about what they are thinking about you, serves nothing.
- Seeking approval is a waste of your time and energy. It will only bring you suffering.
- It's not about whether others approve of you but if YOU approve of you.
- This is what counts.
- Being popular with the world at the expense of your soul is a true booby prize.
- How people perceive you reveals more about themselves than it does about you. People will perceive you based on their own conditioning and filters. So don't take it personally.
- We sometimes hold back being fully ourselves, or stepping out and living our purpose in a big way because of the fear of being judged and what people will think or say.

- Here's the deal: When you put yourself out there in the world, and dare to follow your dreams, it is a risk. It is a vulnerable and courageous act.
- People will judge you.
- People will talk about you.
- People will project their stuff onto you.
- It is what it is.
- In fact some people won't like you. And they don't even know you. This is unavoidable. Make peace with this up front.
- Do not give those that don't even know you the power to determine your happiness.
- Do not give even those that know you the power to determine who you should be and what your limits are.
- Know who you are.
- As you accept yourself as you are and as you are not, you become powerful. You consolidate your energy and remain rooted in your center. You become free.
- When you no longer seek other people's approval you are free. As you unhook yourself from other people's validation, you become truly powerful.
- Your soul is already SELF validated.
- You can please some of the people some of the time but you can't please all the people all of the time. In fact there will be those that, no matter what you do, will think negatively and never be satisfied. This has nothing to do with you.
- Jesus. Bruce Lee. Gandhi. Bob Marley. Martin Luther King Jr. They all had people that didn't like them.
- Remember that there really are no enemies. Just those that don't know you yet and neither themselves.
- At the end of the day you are the one that has to live with yourself.
- Even if you do get others approval, if it's at the expense of yourself, it won't be truly satisfying.

- Trying to get people's approval is a form of control. But in doing so you are the one that ends up controlled.
- The energy it takes is not worth it, as it often requires you give up a part of yourself in order to get the approval.
- It's expensive.
- As I often say, if everyone likes you you might want to be concerned. When you follow your heart you will make waves in this world.
- You will stand out. You will upset some people. You will create change.
- Life is a daring adventure to be lived with no regrets.
- It takes true boldness to be yourself fully.
- People have the right to think whatever they want to think about you.
- Let that be their business.
- So what do you think about you?
- What other people think about you is none of your business!
- Love. Now

—Kute"

CHAPTER TEN
Serving Others Creates Life-Giving Energy!

We Are All Connected

One of life's greatest lessons is coming to the realization that we are not meant to be solo in this life. I am not talking about romance here either. I mean as we travel down this path, we need good high quality friends (much like the good high quality carbs we talked about earlier in the food and nutrition section). Realizing that we are all connected somehow is a pretty powerful concept.

What Will Your Superhero Footprints Look Like?

Who you are today and what you do today can have a big impact on the world you live in! Knowing this is powerful! You are a superhero every single day. You have it in you already. You have the power to think: Your thoughts become words and your words become actions. Your actions become the mark—the footprints, you leave on our world.

PLUGGING IN PRACTICE:
Journal About the Mark You Hope to Leave
on the World

- What kinds of footprints would you like to leave? You can figure this out by tapping into what you are good at.

- What brings you joy? What makes you smile?

- What can you easily do that other people struggle with? What comes naturally to you? This list is endless, but here are a few ideas: organizing spaces, like garages or closets or cupboards; a subject area in school; fix-it projects; bicycle maintenance; computer skills; caring for children or pets; visiting cats at the animal shelter to help socialize them to make them more adoptable; kitchen skills; gardening or yard clean-up; extending hospitality, like those who welcome visitors to a restaurant or a nursing home. What else comes to mind?

- If you could do anything with your time today, what would it be? (Sleep doesn't count here).

Your Gifts Are Within Your Reach

Knowing what brings you joy makes this easier. It took me a long time to figure out that I like to write and that I am good at it. But when I look back now, I have to laugh. I have journalled my whole life. There isn't a time I can think of when I wasn't writing. And I have always loved working with young people. So focusing on these as my passions makes good sense. Your joy doesn't have to be something huge and earth shattering. In fact, the simpler, the better. Tapping into your skills is like tapping into the divine. You have this within your reach and you nurture it and move it forward.

Using Your Gifts Creates a Ripple Effect

So let's use an example. Say for instance, you are really good at math. You know the answer before even working the problem. How can you use your math for good? Do you have a sibling you can help? Imagine if you decided to help your sibling even when she didn't ask for help? Can you envision the positive effects of that? She'll be happy and she'll approach her class with more enthusiasm because she is confident. Her confidence and positive attitude will shine at school and inevitably have a positive effect on a classmate. The ripples are endless.

> **Here are a few more ideas for offering service to others:**
>
> - Have you considered helping in a grade school that may not have enough teacher aides?
>
> - Could you work a day into your life to help out a child? Show a child that you are not there for payment, not there for community service hours, but there to help because you want to be there. Because it is in you to serve others. Now THAT is a pretty powerful message from a strong, positive role model!
>
> - And get this! Can you take this one step further and think about how being good at math might actually hold the key to a fulfilling career?
>
> The key here is finding out what your talent is so that you enjoy what you are doing. This should be easy for you—not something that will create additional stress.

Use Your Gifts for the Greater Good

When we make time for others and we say "yes," amazing things happen inside of us. Remember, we are designed to be with people. We are not in isolation. How can you help? Maybe your schedule just doesn't allow the flexibility to help after school. Okay, when *do* you have time? What can you do? Even the simplest deed has impact. Can you hold a door for someone? Smile in the halls? Unload the dishwasher without being asked? When we see ourselves as a gift, we recognize that our words and deeds can have a positive ripple effect. Our commitment to serve others warms hearts and makes the world a better place.

Expect Nothing But Warm Fuzzies in Return

We also need to be vigilant that when we give of ourselves, we expect nothing in return. We are giving to give. We are giving because it feels good. I guess we do have an expectation of feeling happy. But to keep track, to expect someone to pay back the good deed or act of kindness...that is not giving. That is manipulation. Do good because you can. That is all. Do good because you can. But remember...

- It's not healthy to be a puppet on a string. You will feel it when you are being used and manipulated by someone taking advantage or by toxic others.

- Speaking of string, we give with no strings attached; we do not expect anything in return.

EXCEPTION! Add this volunteer activity on a part-time job application or college application!

Consider writing about this activity as part of a college application essay or supplemental essay. Also, be sure to list it when you apply for a part time job. Pay or no pay, your willingness to volunteer shows moxy!

Feeling Compassion Helps to Lift Our Mood

One of the quickest ways to get out of a bad mood is to see firsthand how others who are less fortunate live, often with gratitude for simpler things in life. There are very few times in life where I feel comparing is okay. This is one of them. I make the exception because when you start to look beyond yourself and your life, you gain perspective. Also, sometimes when we focus too heavily on just ourselves, we neglect to see how others feel. One of my students who had always been caught up in drama spent time as a counselor at a camp for kids with disabilities. The experience transformed his life. The kids changed him. When he worked with them, he felt their joy, and it changed his perspective on what's really important in life.

Those close to us also have challenges. Without enabling, what can you do to lift them up? How can you lighten their load? What kind of a positive footprint do you want to leave on this individual's life?

Use Your Gifts Every Day in Service to Others

In Chapter I, you worked through a few exercises to help identify one or more of your innate passions and gifts. When this gift helps lead you to your vocational calling, it can become your gift to the world. However, starting now, you have an opportunity every day to make a difference through community service or small gestures.

Keep Community Service Simple!

So many places in the community need your help. I know of a young girl who goes with her mother every weekend to help muck horse stalls at an equine therapy program. Yes, she's scooping horse manure and it's really is a big deal! Maintaining clean stalls helps keep the animals healthy and happy!

PLUGGING IN PRACTICE:
Cluster or Brainstorm on Paper a
Few Places to Volunteer

Clustering is another way to think of new ideas. Take a clean sheet of paper. In the center, in a small circle, write "Places to Volunteer." Then set a timer or look at your watch. Give yourself 5 minutes to jot every person or organization in your area that could use your help. This is a "First Thought, Best Thought," activity, so do not take too long to think, and do not censor yourself. Your topic, words and phrases will be different from the ones in the clustering sample here, but format-wise, your cluster might end up looking similar.

- Look over your cluster and put an asterisk next to your favorite 3-4 ideas.

- Jot these 3-4 ideas on a sheet of paper along with organizations/places in your city or town that offer the kind of volunteer opportunities you seek.

- Review their websites to learn more and to find contact information for the volunteer coordinator.

- Call or email the volunteer coordinator to arrange a visit to learn more about volunteer activities, and to complete volunteer paperwork. Many places also offer training.

- If your clustering did not help you to brainstorm ideas, then select a volunteer activity from this list:

Try a food pantry

A homeless shelter

An animal hospital or animal shelter

A local school

Do you have an elderly neighbor who would enjoy a visit once a week?

Maybe you could do a word search with a senior or a crossword puzzle.

Do you have old drawings or sketches you could bring to a senior living facility? Offer your drawings to the nurses and ask if they know of a resident who could use a little color in their room.

Can you play the piano? Go ask if you can hop in and play for an hour or so. People love music. It makes their soul dance. How cool would you feel inside if you knew you made the heart of a sweet elderly man sing because you took the time to play a few songs?

- Make an appointment to learn more about the place you'd like to volunteer.

- Call to arrange a visit or to attend volunteer orientation, if this is a requirement.

- Commit to volunteer once a week or twice a month.

Commit to What You Can Manage...Even If *"Only"* Random Acts of Kindness

Again, this doesn't have to be huge. Community service should not bring stress. It's important for you to maintain balance in your life!

Endless opportunities wait for you as you awaken each day!

If a volunteer position feels like too much right now, you can still make a difference. Young adults and teens like to go places- shopping, movies, restaurants. The next time you are out and about, look for opportunities for random acts of kindness. Fore example, take the time to leave your phone (hidden) in your car or pocket, so that you can look at the cashier and smile. Remember what it mean to use your manners. Hold doors for people. Be kind to the servers in the restaurants you patronize.

Remember, each of us has a desire to feel loved and appreciated. You can do your part by simply saying *hello, thank you,* and *have a good day.* It isn't hard. Believe me when I tell you that your heart feels happier, your steps are lighter and your kindness will ripple.

PLUGGING IN PRACTICE:
Your Volunteer Experience—Reflect in Your Journal

A couple of weeks after adopting your "community service" and "random acts of kindness" mindset, write about the following:

- What new activity has brought the most joy to you? Why?

- How does your service activity make use of your best qualities?

- Do you feel any connection to your chosen service and your vocational calling, or what you might like to do in your future career?

- Has any part of this process been frustrating? If so, what could make it better next time?

CHAPTER ELEVEN
The Power of Vulnerability

"To share your weakness is to make yourself vulnerable; to make
yourself vulnerable is to show your strength."
—*Criss Jami*[31]

A super important message I try to convey in my classes is that it is okay to be wrong, to make mistakes and to not know. We as a culture detest not knowing. I have seen students hide their uncertainty time and again. Here's how it goes: A student asks a question. I answer, and a blank look comes over their face. They nod and confirm they understand. But I know better. They are just as confused as they were before they asked. Why don't they say, "No, I don't get it. This still doesn't make sense"? Because to admit uncertainty makes us feel vulnerable. We think vulnerable means "weak." Weak means you are on the outside. No one wants to be on the outside.

Vulnerability Is Your Greatest Asset on the Road to Success
You know what I think? I think vulnerability is beautiful. I think being vulnerable and *admitting you do not know or understand* means you are willing to take chances; you are confident no matter the outcome; willing to put in tremendous effort. Trust me, you do this and you will grow.

Being vulnerable also means being authentic. Vulnerable means you find yourself real and human and flawed. That's also beautiful. That means you have a vision of yourself that is true and authentic.

I love that.

Our culture tells us that someone who is vulnerable is a weak, meek little person who won't speak up for herself because she thinks she isn't worth it. Well, just like we reframed the concept of "failure," it's time to redefine "vulnerable."

Technically, the definition of "vulnerable" is to wound, hurt, injure or maim. All negative connotations, so it's no wonder people balk at feeling vulnerable. Let's look at how author Stephen Russell puts this definition into context:

> "Vulnerability is the only authentic state. Being vulnerable means being open, for wounding, but also for pleasure. Being open to the wounds of life means also being open to the bounty and beauty. Don't mask or deny your vulnerability: it is your greatest asset. Be vulnerable: quake and shake in your boots with it. The new goodness that is coming to you, in the form of people, situations, and things can only come to you when you are vulnerable, i.e. open."

> —Stephen Russell, *Barefoot Doctor's Guide to the Tao: A Spiritual Handbook for the Urban Warrior*[32]

To be vulnerable, he says, is to be open for wounding...but that's not where we remain. This is a good time to remember that amazing quotation by 16th century poet and mystic Rumi: "The wound is the place where the light enters you." By being open, we also open to beauty, bounty, pleasure and light. New wisdom and growth. So our wounding ultimately leads us to a higher good.

Being Vulnerable Takes Courage

I had a student who was fearful of asking a question in front of the whole class. She wanted to ask me privately, even though her question did not involve a personal issue. To move her beyond fear, I encouraged her to allow me to guide her through the following steps:

1. I asked her to close her eyes and tap into how she was feeling about asking the question.
2. Then I asked her if that was a real feeling or imagined.
3. We talked about how being afraid or feeling vulnerable is usually our lower self that keeps us from learning and moving forward.
4. I asked her to ignore those negative feelings for now and to proceed with the question.
5. Afterwards, we talked about how she felt by pushing through.
6. She learned that asking wasn't that bad after all; she had a new strength and was in the process of learning to trust what she needed for her growth.

Asking Questions Shows You Are Curious

You see, when we choose not to ask questions for fear of looking dumb or inadequate, we are worried about the external views, about what others think. Let's remember...what others think is none of our business! What matters is our goal. We will meet these goals when we have the courage to take chances. So dare to be curious and to ask those questions! There is growth in asking. You will gain confidence as you slowly strip away the fear of being vulnerable. With practice, asking for help will feel like a natural part of your growth process.

Author and researcher Brene Brown said, "Vulnerability is the absolute heartbeat of innovation and creativity."[33] Albert Einstein said, "I have no special talents. I am only passionately curious."[34] So, in fact, what you learn by asking questions, by being passionately curious, may help you to be more creative and to land far beyond your original question!

I might add that the student who finally asked her question, did so in front of 23 other students. Afterwards, she felt empowered. I have created an environment in my classroom of tolerance, acceptance, and love. My kids know I have their best interests at heart. Subsequently, they take risks because they trust I will be there for them throughout the process.

Asking a Question in Class Encourages Others to Do the Same
What happened afterwards was transformational. My students began asking more questions, seeking more answers (often not related to the subject at hand, but still, amazing questions), and daring to be vulnerable. They grasped the connection between asking for help and success.

If You Do Not Feel Like You Have a Supportive Environment
So what do you do if you don't have a teacher with whom you can be vulnerable? Keep reading. I have some thoughts on this for you in the practice section that follows. Remember one of our lessons is to recognize that we don't get to change other people. We can only shape our own thoughts, feelings and actions. The following is a guide for you to follow regardless of your learning environment.

PLUGGING IN PRACTICE:
Overcome Barriers to Achieve Your Goals

- Create a goal. Write it down in several places—sticky notes, planners, calendars, wherever you will see it and see it often.

  a. Ask yourself: What do I already know that can help me to reach this goal?

  b. What is the next step for this goal?

  c. In what areas will I need to improve to reach this goal?

- Identify Ways to Support Your Process

  a. Formulate a list of people you can ask for help.

  b. Reach out and ask them for help! When you have the courage and the ability to ask in person, people have a harder time saying no, so long as you are respectful and ask to meet at a convenient time.

  c. Use prayer or meditation and ask for pure, clear guidance. Copy meaningful, inspiring passages that you can access several times a day.

  d. Be in tune to the goal throughout the process. Stay focused and "Keep your eye on the prize."

  e. Listen to the advice or the help that you receive.

- If your goal changes, have the courage to alter your path.

- Once you have reached your goal or you feel you have completed the process, review the process. Write the following in your journal:

  a. What felt easy about this process?

b. What parts were most difficult for you and why?

c. Identify the areas where you would like to improve.

d. Identify the areas where you felt successful.

- Look inward as you reflect on this process of working toward your goals. Write in your journal:

a. Where are you starting to push through on your blocks?

b. Have you been able to identify the areas in your life that tend to hold you back?

c. How can you continue to shred those areas and rebuild them?

Feel good about yourself knowing that being vulnerable also means showing strength and courage, which helps you to tackle many things in life and to reach your goals. Remember that this is YOUR path. What others think (as long as you are working for the higher good) is not important. Zhang Xin CEO of real estate company SOHO China decided as a teen to reach for a better life. She worked in factories for five years and attended night school before saving up enough to attend university in England. The advice she has for her younger self: "Oh, just go for it. Go for your dream, whatever dream you have. And don't (be) worried about (what) people think. (If they say) 'This is ridiculous,' often it's the most ridiculous ideas that turn out to be the best."[35]

Your work and your reputation will take care of the naysayers. Remember, too, that you have the guidance from the divine. You can succeed and you will. You have to do the work, but you also have to trust that if you are genuine in your approach, bigger and better will come of this work.

CHAPTER TWELVE
Mindful Meditation
Getting to Know You

Misunderstandings About Meditation

What do you picture when someone uses the word *meditation*? Do you picture people humming mantras as they sit cross-legged at the peak of a cliff overlooking the Himalayan Mountains?

This is a gross misperception. You do not have to leave your house. You do not even have to silence your mind. Also, meditation is not religion.

Meditation takes practice, but it is not difficult. And yes, you might feel awkward at first. I sure did!

When I took a mediation class years ago, here is what I experienced: I felt awkward, totally uncomfortable and out of place. Instead of keeping my eyes closed, I kept peeking out of my right eye to see if anyone else was staring around the room, feeling out of step, like I was.

Nope. Just me. Not being in the moment. (I was in the other moment—my own untrusting, worry, ego-driven questioning moment!) I honestly had to resist bursting out in laughter, because I was so sure that I didn't really fit in. It took me nearly 20 years to try again.

In retrospect, I learned from that experience that there is no one right or wrong way to meditate. You do not have to swear off your everyday life, head for the Himalayans, and adopt a solitary lifestyle. Not at all.

What is Meditation?

Meditation is the art of being still and listening to your mind, body and spirit. It's a fascinating way to help you to know yourself better, what you are about, and how to make the most of your life on a daily basis...by moving mindfully through life.

Types of Meditation

I've learned that meditation comes in many forms. It can involve slow movement and gentle breathing (like Tai Chi, Yoga and Qigong). Some people appreciate Walking Meditation as a way to cultivate mindfulness and awareness of being in the moment. Meditation can involve stillness, like sitting quietly while visualizing or saying mantras. Meditation can also involve reflection.

You Decide and Customize...So Long as It Brings You Peace

The point is YOU get to decide how to create a meditation program that will work for you. I had to let go of the idea that I was "doing it wrong." In time, I realized that simply slowing and quieting down, even if just for five minutes, is a form of meditation. I also realized that going about my chores and daily work with greater awareness and presence is also a form of meditation. We call this "mindfulness" or being "mindful."

Today, I incorporate meditation into my daily routine. It's really a beautiful experience once you begin to practice doing so. The benefits of meditation are tremendous. Your heart rate slows, your muscles relax, you feel peace and clarity. Sometimes I meditate twice a day!

Where Do I Start? Search Terms & Link

Find a mediation online. Amazon Prime, Netflix and YouTube have excellent ones. Just search for what you're looking for. Meditation for Beginners, Morning Meditation, Guided Meditation for Restful Sleep. Ten minutes, half hour, one hour. They literally have hundreds for free from which to choose. To begin, I suggest that you search for a guided, short meditation from a reputable source, so that the speaker can walk you through the experience and help you to quiet or clear your mind. Here is a link to eight free guided meditations to stream or download offered by the U.C.L.A.[36] http://marc.ucla.edu/mindful-meditations. They are in English and also in Spanish.

As you practice and become better at this, you can work through meditation on your own. Blue Mountain Center of Meditation also offers truly life-enhancing passage meditation.[37] You can learn more at **https://www.bmcm.org/learn/**

How I Customized My Meditation Practice

So first find the meditation that works for you. I sometimes play one and get about five minutes in and feel like it's just not for me. No big deal; I choose another one. You might enjoy something calm. My friend swears by the same kind of soothing music she found on Youtube for her cats. You heard that right! (**https://www.youtube.com/watch?v=VGu_VZjaRog**)[38] No drums or synthesizers, so really great for winding down. One that I absolutely love to play in the morning is called "Morning Rampage" by Esther Hicks. If you search for it, you will most likely find it under the name Abraham Hicks, a name she also uses. The high frequency vibrational music and her voice calling out and affirming that it's really going to be a great day always leave me with a smile. I honestly cannot think of a day when I played this and left the house feeling grumpy.

I also play this while I have my sun lamp on. In the Midwest, the winters can be brutal and the gray days are relentless. This can take a toll on anyone's spirit. So I protect my spirit and I use the lamp to get some artificial sun in my life. The lamp was a Christmas gift from my husband, and I use it every day.

Before you begin, make sure you wear comfortable clothes. It's tough to meditate if your belt is digging in, or you have an itchy tag on the back of your shirt.

Find a quiet, comfortable space or nook where you will not be interrupted for the duration of the meditation. If you have a busy household, I strongly recommend using your earbuds to minimize any distractions. You want to get the most out of this gift of time with yourself.

Many guided online meditations will come with beautiful images or scenery; if you care to watch, feel free. I like to close my eyes and create my own images.

Walking as Meditation

Another way I like to meditate is to take a walk in the woods behind my house. I can feel the sun poking through the trees, the snap of the branches quietly underfoot, the birds call out in a choir to me. The shift I feel inside of me feels very calming and my purpose in life becomes clearer. I feel like the universe is guiding me along in my thoughts and truly supports me. It's magical really and something I don't get when I am sitting on the floor in my room. Even as a teenager, I was drawn to Thoreau's love for nature and how spending time in nature helps us to look inward and to feel more self-reliant. In his famous essay, he begins, "I went to the woods because I wished to live deliberately."

What is Forest Bathing and Yes! By All Means, Keep Your Clothes ON!

Doctors now prescribe "Forest Bathing," directing patients to spend time outside in nature as a way to find greater peace inside and to break free from digital distractions. Forest therapy was developed in Japan during the 1980s and has become a foundation of preventive health care and healing in Japanese medicine.[39] If you opt to try this, go someplace safe, familiar and populated. Your yard is also an option. Scientists have proven that forest bathing reduces inflammation, stress, depression and anger, while optimizing cardiovascular health, immune function, cognitive function and creativity! It also offers a deeper connection to nature. Thoreau would have approved!

Let's Get Started!

You do not need anything else to benefit from meditation. But everyone is free to do what works best. So, one other component I add is my oil diffuser. I found a good, reliable one at the local drugstore that came with oils, for a total cost of under $15.00. I have friends who are sensitive to aromas, or who have sensitive pets. For this reason, they do not use diffusers.

So in my comfy clothes, in a quiet space, with my oil diffuser humming away, I hit "play," and my program begins. During my meditation time, I allow myself to let go of all the stress and anxiety in my life. If my mind wanders, I allow it to do so. This is not about being perfect. This is "a date" with your spirit. After a few moments, I gently pull my thoughts back to the meditation. I feel my breaths coming in and I feel them going out. I bless myself. I tell myself how lucky I am to be alive. I tell myself that no matter what, I am always granted a new, fresh beginning to my day- even if it's four o'clock in the afternoon! I use this time to feel gratitude in my heart. When I adopt an attitude of gratitude, I feel lighter and my problems are minimized.

Benefits of Meditation

Studies have indicated that people who practice meditation and mindful thinking have increased immune systems, less stress and cortisol, improves sleep and reduces insomnia, decreased inflammation in the body, reduced pain and improved mood and more happiness.

The immediate benefits from practicing this *even once a day for five minutes* are awesome! You will feel calmer, your heart rate will slow down, you will have a clearer picture of what you desire. You begin to recognize how positive thinking makes you feel better physically! Not a bad deal for a free tool that you carry right in your own mind and body!

PLUGGING IN PRACTICE:
Your Meditation Practice

- **Gather some resources.** Go to your local library and browse through the section offering books and cd's on mindfulness, meditation, and positive affirmations. Check out several to use as you begin your new practice.

- **Find a comfortable space.** Find a corner in your room or your house with a comfortable chair, corner of the sofa, or with space for a floor cushion. Establish this as your meditation "go-to" space. Equip it with what you might need: a quilt or afghan for chilly days, some way to play music or guided meditations, affirmation books or readings.

- **Commit** to meditating for at least five minutes for the next seven days.

  –Sit or lie comfortably.

  –Close your eyes.

  –Breathe naturally.

  –Focus on each breath and observe how your body moves with each inhalation and exhalation.

PLUGGING IN PRACTICE:
Journaling for Self-Reflection:
After Meditation Practice

Reflect & Write

- Notice how you now feel compared to how you felt before your meditation.

- **Write in Your Journal:** After each session, take some time to jot a few notes about your mood. What is different? Can you feel a shift in your attitude? How do you feel now as compared to when you first began? Again, this is not about feeling a HUGE change. This is a little by little gain that increases the more your practice.

WORKS CITED

Chapter 1: Find Your Meaning in Life

1. Whyte, David. 2018. "David Whyte Quote". *A-Z Quotes*. http://www.azquotes.com/quote/797976. Accessed July 14, 2018.

2. Hillman, James. 1996. *The Soul's Code*. New York: Random House.

3. Gardner, Howard. 1993. *Multiple Intelligences, The Theory In Practice*. New York: BasicBooks.

4. "Theory Of Multiple Intelligences". 2018. *En.Wikipedia.Org*. https://en.wikipedia.org/wiki/Theory_of_multiple_intelligences. Accessed July 14, 2018.

5. Thatchenkery, Tojo, and Carol Metzker. 2006. *Appreciativeintelligence. Com*. http://www.appreciativeintelligence.com/articles/Article%204. pdf. Accessed July 14, 2018.

Chapter 2: Moving Through Sadness

6. "NIMH » Major Depression". 2018. *Nimh.Nih.Gov*. https://www. nimh.nih.gov/health/statistics/major-depression.shtml. Accessed July 14, 2018.

7. Forgas, Joseph. 2014. "Four Ways Sadness May Be Good For You". *Greater Good*. https://greatergood.berkeley.edu/article/item/four_ways_sadness_may_be_good_for_you. Accessed July 14, 2018.

8. Howes, Lewis. 2015. *The School Of Greatness: A Real-World Guide To Living Bigger, Loving Deeper, And Leaving A Legacy*. Rodale Books.

Chapter 3: Healthy Alternatives to Stuffing, Drugs and Alcohol

9. "NIMH » Major Depression". 2018.

10. Soat, Molly. 2018. "Social Media Triggers A Dopamine High". *Ama.Org*. Accessed July 14. https://www.ama.org/publications/ MarketingNews/Pages/feeding-the-addiction.aspx. Accessed July 14, 2018.

11. Richard, Jocelyn. 2012. "Web Addiction Similar To Alcoholism? Study Says Yes". *Huffpost UK*. https://www.huffingtonpost. com/2012/01/12/web-addicts-brain-chemistry-addiction-alcoholics-gamblers_n_1202480.html. Accessed July 14, 2018.

12. Hales, Lydia. 2015. "Understanding Sleepy Teens - Health & Wellbeing". *ABC Health & Wellbeing*. http://www.abc.net.au/health/ features/stories/2015/05/21/4239985.htm. Accessed July 14, 2018.

Chapter 4: Move It, Shake It, for Optimal Well-Being

13. "Moving On At Finestquotes.Com". 2018. *Finestquotes*. https://www. finestquotes.com/author_quotes-author-Hans%20Bos-page-0.htm. Accessed July 14, 2018.

14. "History Of Laughter Yoga - Laughter Yoga University". 2018. *Laughter Yoga University*. Accessed July 14. https://laughteryoga.org/ history-of-laughter-yoga/. Accessed July 14, 2018.

15. Dunbar, R. I. M., R. Baron, A. Frangou, E. Pearce, E. J. C. van Leeuwen, J. Stow, G. Partridge, I. MacDonald, V. Barra, and M. van Vugt. 2011. "Social Laughter Is Correlated With An Elevated Pain Threshold". *Proceedings Of The Royal Society B: Biological Sciences* 279 (1731).

16. Bratman, Gregory N., J. Paul Hamilton, Kevin S. Hahn, Gretchen C. Daily, and James J. Gross. 2015. "Nature Experience Reduces Rumination And Subgenual Prefrontal Cortex Activation". *Proceedings Of The National Academy Of Sciences* 112 (28): 8567-8572.

17. Greenberg, Melanie. 2017. "Stuck In Negative Thinking? It Could Be Your Brain". *Psychology Today*. https://www.psychologytoday.com/gb/comment/947974. Accessed July 14, 2018.

Chapter 5: Reframing Our Greatest Learning Tools: Mistakes & Failure

18. Leonard, Thomas J. 1999. *The Portable Coach*. London: Simon & Schuster.

19. Waitley, Denis. 2018. "Forget about the consequences of failure. Failure is only a temporary change in direction to set you straight for your next success." "Denis Waitley Quotes". Brainyquote. https://www.brainyquote.com/quotes/denis_waitley_125741. Accessed July 14, 2018.

Chapter 6: The Food → Mood Connection: Take Charge of Your Cravings!

20. Longo, Natasha. 2013. "Listen To Your Body: What Food Cravings Are Telling You". *Thehealersjournal.Com*. http://www.thehealersjournal.com/2013/08/27/listen-to-your-body-food-cravings/.

21. Bellum, Sara. 2014. "The Buzz On Caffeine". *NIDA For Teens*. https://teens.drugabuse.gov/blog/post/buzz-caffeine-updated. Accessed July 14, 2018.

22. Byrne, Rhonda. 2006. *Secret, The*. New York: Atria Books.

Chapter 7: Social Media Aside, Learn to "Like" Your Irresistible Self!

23. Soat, Molly. 2018.

24. Kaiser, Shannon. 2017. "3 Unexpected Ways To Find Your Life Purpose". *Huffpost*. https://www.huffingtonpost.com/shannon-kaiser/3-unexpected-ways-to-find_b_5176511.html. Accessed July 14, 2018.

Chapter 8: Self Love Sets Foundation for Positive Changes in Your Life

25. McMaster Bujold, Lois. 2018. "Lois Mcmaster Bujold Quotes At Quotes 2 Know". *Quotes 2 Know*. Accessed July 14. https://www.quotes2know.com/Lois-McMaster-Bujold-Quotes/115994. Accessed July 14, 2018.

26. "Maya Angelou Quotes: 15 Of The Best". 2014. https://www.theguardian.com/books/2014/may/28/maya-angelou-in-fifteen-quotes. Accessed July 14, 2018.

Chapter 9: How Best to Deal With Negative—*Toxic*—People and Comments

27. Raghunathan, Rajraj. 2013. "Dealing With Negative People". *Psychology Today*. https://www.psychologytoday.com/us/blog/sapient-nature/201303/dealing-negative-people. Accessed July 14, 2018.

28. Chopra, Deepak. 2018. "Deepak Chopra Quote: "What Other People Think Of You Is Not Your Business."". *Quotefancy.Com*. https://quotefancy.com/quote/792480/Deepak-Chopra-What-other-people-think-of-you-is-not-your-business-If-you-start-to-make. Accessed July 14, 2018.

29. Blackson, Kute. 2018. "What Other People Think Of You Is None Of Your Business". Blog. *K.* Accessed July 14. http://kuteblackson. com/blog/?p=1235. Accessed July 14, 2018.

Chapter 10: Serving Others Creates Life-Giving Energy

30. *Writing Tips: Clustering.* 2018. Image. Accessed July 14. https://web2.uvcs.uvic.ca/elc/sample/beginner/wt/wt_04.htm. Accessed July 14, 2018.

Chapter 11: The Power of Vulnerability

31. Jami, Criss. 2018. "Criss Jami Quote - To Share Your Weakness Is To Make Yourse... | Quote Catalog". *Quotecatalog.Com.* Accessed July 14. https://quotecatalog.com/quote/criss-jami-to-share-your-w-G7PvLma/. Accessed July 14, 2018.

32. Russell, Stephen. 1998. *Barefoot Doctor's Guide To The Tao.* New York: Times Books.

33. Weisul, Kimberly. 2013. "Why The Best Leaders Are Vulnerable". *Inc.Com.* https://www.inc.com/kimberly-weisul/leadership-why-the-best-leaders-are-vulnerable.html. Accessed July 14, 2018.

34. Einstein, Albert. "Albert Einstein Quotes". *Brainyquote.* https://www.brainyquote.com/quotes/albert_einstein_174001. Accessed July 14, 2018.

35. Handley, Lucy. 2017. "4 Top Ceos Reveal All About Their 'Terrible' And 'Socially Challenged' Teenage Years". *CNBC.* https://www.cnbc.com/2017/08/29/ceos-awkward-teenage-years-and-how-they-became-successful.html. Accessed July 14, 2018.

Chapter 12: Mindful Meditation—Getting to Know You

36. "Guided Meditations—UCLA Mindful Awareness Research Center —Los Angeles, CA". 2018. *Marc.Ucla.Edu*. Accessed July 17. http://marc.ucla.edu/mindful-meditations. Accessed July 14, 2018.

37. "Learn". 2018. *Bmcm.Org*. Accessed July 17. https://www.bmcm.org/learn/. Accessed July 14, 2018.

38. "2 Hours Of Cat Sleeping Music- RELAXING MUSIC FOR CATS - 2 HORA GATO MÚSICA - RELAXING SOUNDS". 2015. *Youtube*. https://www.youtube.com/watch?v=VGu_VZjaRog. Accessed on July 18, 2018.

39. "Shinrin-Yoku Forest Medicine". 2018. *Shinrin-Yoku: The Medicine Of Being In The Forest*. http://www.shinrin-yoku.org/shinrin-yoku.html. Accessed July 14, 2018.